God's
Blueprint
for
Marriage
&
Family

by

David L. Brown, Ph.D.

Disclaimer

The author of this work has quoted the writers of many articles and books. This does not mean that the author endorses or recommends the works of others. If the author quotes someone, it does not mean that he agrees with all of the author's tenets, statements, concepts, or words, whether in the work quoted or any other work of the author. There has been no attempt to alter the meaning of the quotes; and therefore, some of the quotes are long in order to give the entire sense of the passage.

† **†** †

Dr. David L Brown

P.O. Box 173
Oak Creek, Wisconsin 53154
PastorDavidLBrown@gmail.com
© 1984, 2017 by David L. Brown

Printed in the United States of America
REL006201: Religion: Biblical Studies - Topical

ISBN 978-0-9993545-4-4

All Scripture quotes are from the King James Bible except those verses compared and then the source is identified.

Address All Inquiries To:
THE OLD PATHS PUBLICATIONS, Inc.
142 Gold Flume Way
Cleveland, Georgia, 30528
U.S.A.
Web: www.theoldpathspublications.com
E-mail: TOP@theoldpathspublications.com

1.0

DEDICATION

I dedicate this book to my wife Linda. I am a blessed man to have a wife like her. We were married young. She was 19 and I was 20. We both loved the Lord and wanted to serve him together, and we, as a team, have done that for almost 50 years! However, we both found out very quickly that making a marriage work takes WORK! You do not just say "I Do" and live happily ever after. Marriage requires commitment to the Lord and commitment to each other because there are no perfect husbands and no perfect wives.

I would also like to dedicate this book to Ellen Blount, Linda's mother. She prepared Linda to be a good wife and mother. I have written this book to share with you some of the things that have helped us to keep our marriage from becoming a cold utilitarian relationship.

David L. Brown

"Let every one of you in particular so love his wife even as himself; and the wife see that she reverence her husband." **Ephesians 5:33**

Included are chapters on...

God's Blueprint For Husbands
God's Blueprint For Wives
God's Blueprint For Communication
God's Blueprint For Commitment
God's Blueprint For Parents
God's Blueprint For Children

TABLE OF CONTENTS

Keep The Home Fires Burning

CHAPTER 1
TEXT: GENESIS 2:18-25

There is one key statement about marriage that occurs four times in the Bible. To my knowledge, this is the only statement about marriage that God includes four times in the Bible. Let's take a look at this statement –

- **Genesis 2:24** *Therefore shall a man leave his father and his mother, and shall cleave unto his wife: and they shall be one flesh.*
- **Matthew 19:5** *And said, For this cause shall a man leave father and mother, and shall cleave to his wife: and they twain shall be one flesh?*
- **Mark 10:7-8** *For this cause shall a man leave his father and mother, and cleave to his wife; 8 And they twain shall be one flesh: so then they are no more twain, but one flesh.*
- **Ephesians 5:31** *For this cause shall a man leave his father and mother, and shall be joined unto his wife, and they two shall be one flesh.*

The outline for this chapter is going to focus on the three recurring statements in these verses... *leave, cleave,* and *one flesh*. Since God so often repeated these things, once before man fell into sin and three times after he fell into sin, I believe God's blueprint for marriage can be found within these verses.

Outline – God's Blueprint For Marriage

Leave -- Husbands & Wives Are Directed **To Leave** Their Fathers and Mothers!
Cleave – Husbands & Wives Are Directed **To Cleave** To One Another
One Flesh – Husbands & Wives Are Directed To An Exclusive One Flesh Relationship

---

✓ LEAVE

HUSBANDS AND WIVES ARE DIRECTED TO LEAVE THEIR FATHERS AND MOTHERS!

What It Does NOT Mean

1. **It does not mean you ignore, abandon or forsake your parents** – Mark 7:9-13 makes that clear that God does not approve of this!
2. 1Timothy 5:4,8 indicates a special responsibility for children and close relatives to care for the widows in the family.
3. **It does not mean that you must make a move away from the vicinity in which your parents live** – "Living too close to parents at the beginning of a marriage may make it more difficult to leave, but it is possible to leave your father and mother and still live next door. Conversely, it is possible to live a thousand miles away from your parents and not leave them. In fact, you may not have left your parents even though they are dead." *(Strengthening Your Marriage* by Wayne Mack, page 1)

What It DOES Mean

Once you are married there is to be a fundamental change in your relationship with your parents. Leaving your parents means…

1. **The husband-wife relationship is now the priority relationship** – Your relationship with your parents must now take a back seat to your relationship with your spouse. In fact, all other relationships must now be secondary.

10

2. **It means that you are more concerned about your spouse's ideas, opinions, and directives than you are of your parents** – Some times there is a power struggle between the two sets of parents. A husband and wife must be careful that they do not allow the parents to manipulate them.

3. **It means you must not try to change your mate simply because your parents do not like something about him or her.**

4. **It means that you are not primarily dependent on your parents for finances, affection, approval, council, etc.**

Pointers For Parents

Parents, your goal should be to prepare your children to leave, not to stay. As they advance toward maturity you should train them to be independent of you, not dependent on you. Teach them to be decision makers and to manage their money carefully.

Husbands and wives make your mate your best friend, not your children. Don't become too emotionally dependent on your children. As your kids get older be sure to cultivate common interests with your mate. Learn to do things together and deepen your friendship together. Parents who make their children "their life" are in for difficult times when they leave the nest. I'm not saying to ignore your children, but I am saying they should be second and your spouse should be first.

When your children have married, don't try to run their lives! Don't criticize their spouse. You must allow the husband to be the head of his home, to make decisions for himself, to look to his wife, not you, as his helper and his responsibility. You must encourage your daughter to look to her husband for companionship, encouragement, affection, guidance, etc.

✓CLEAVE

Husbands And Wives Are Directed To Cleave To One Another! The Hebrew word translated *cleave* in **Genesis 2:24** is dabaq (daw-bak'; 1692), which means to adhere, stick or be joined together. The Greek word translated *cleave* or *join to* in the New Testament passages is proskollao, (pros-kol-lah'-o; 4347), which means to glue to. Marriage glues two people together!

Look at **Mark 10:7-9** *For this cause shall a man leave his father and mother, and cleave to his wife; 8 And they twain shall be one flesh: so then they are no more twain, but one flesh. 9 What therefore God hath joined together, let not man put asunder.* God planned marriage to be permanent. It is a vow until death do we part! Dr. Wayne Mack says this of marriage – "Marriage means that a husband and wife enter into a relationship for which they accept full responsibility and in which they commit themselves to each other regardless of what problems arise." Marriage is an irrevocable covenant or contract to which we are bound. God is clear about that. **Malachi 2:14** says; *Yet ye say, Wherefore? Because the LORD hath been witness between thee and the wife of thy youth, against whom thou hast dealt treacherously: yet is she thy companion, and the wife of thy covenant.* (See also **Romans 7:2-3; Matthew 19:8-10**)

God's kind of marriage involves a total and irrevocable commitment of two people to each other in good times and in bad times, agreements and disagreements, in joy or in sorrow, in sickness or in health.

God's kind of marriage means that people know that they must face problems, discuss them, seek God's help in them, resolve them rather than run from them, because there is no

12

CHAPTER 1: GENESIS 2:18-25

way out. They are committed to one another for life. They must cleave to one another today and tomorrow, as long as they both shall live. So, work at keeping your marriage strong!

✓ONE FLESH

Husbands And Wives Are Directed To An Exclusive One-Flesh Relationship. Becoming one flesh involves the act of marriage but is more than just that physical act. Within the bounds of marriage and only within that boundary the sexual relationship is holy, beautiful and good (see **Hebrews 13:4; Proverbs 5:18-19**). A husband and wife are a team. Each is to be as concerned about the other's needs as he/she is about their own (**Ephesians 5:28; Proverbs 31:12 & 27**).

God's Blueprint for Marriage – Leave, Cleave And Be One Flesh! [Adapted From *Strengthening Your Marriage* by Wayne Mack]

CHAPTER 2
GOD'S BLUEPRINT FOR HUSBANDS

EXPLANATION & OVERVIEW

The goal of marriage, according to the Bible is completeness, oneness and unity. **Genesis 2:24** says, *Therefore shall a man leave his father and his mother, and shall cleave unto his wife: and they shall be one flesh.* (See also Matthew 19:5; Mark 10:6-9; Ephesians 5:31). In order to achieve this oneness or unity in a marriage the husband must know and fulfill his biblical role and the wife must know and fulfill her biblical role. The problem is that there is mass confusion and chaos today concerning what the role of the husband is and what the role of the wife is in the marital relationship.

Can you imagine the utter confusion that would exist on a football team if the players did not know what their specific responsibilities were? Or, picture the chaos and frustration in a business where there are no job descriptions, where everything is everybody's business and nothing is anybody's business, where everyone is a "chief" and no one is an "Indian". This is the kind of confusion, chaos and frustration that exists in many marriages today because there has never been a sorting out of the responsibilities. The Bible defines the wife's God-given responsibilities to her husband as well as the husband's God-given responsibilities to his wife. In this section we are going to focus on a husband's responsibility to his wife.

A HUSBAND'S TWO KEY RESPONSIBILITIES TO HIS WIFE:

1) **He is to love her**
2) **He is to lead her**

Let's look at the **first** point...

1) A HUSBAND IS RESPONSIBLE TO LOVE HIS WIFE

The wife has such a great need for love or the husband has such a great lack of love, that God commands the husband to love his wife three times within the space of a few verses in **Ephesians 5.** Twice husbands are instructed to love their wives as themselves and once as Christ loved the church.

Ephesians 5:25 *Husbands, love your wives, even as Christ also loved the church, and gave himself for it;*

Ephesians 5:28 *So ought men to love their wives as their own bodies. He that loveth his wife loveth himself.*

Ephesians 5:33 *Nevertheless let every one of you in particular so love his wife even as himself; and the wife see that she reverence her husband.*

We men usually spend a great deal of time, money and effort on ourselves. Our own desires and comforts are very important to us. When we are hungry, we eat. When we are thirsty, we drink. When we are tired, we sleep. When we want our "toys" we buy them. When we want entertainment we turn on the TV or DVD's. Very naturally and carefully and fervently we nourish and cherish ourselves.

TIME OUT!!! Men, the Scripture indicates, the true way a man is to love his wife. He is to nourish her, cherish her, protect her, satisfy her, provide for her, care for her, sacrifice for her to the same degree and extent, and in the same manner as he does himself. Scripture also says, *So ought men to love their wives as their own bodies. He that loveth his wife loveth himself. 29 For no man ever yet hated his own flesh; but nourisheth and cherisheth it, even as the Lord the church:* **Ephesians 5:28-29** *"Husbands, love your wives just as Christ also loved the church."* **Ephesians 5:25**

How did Christ love the church? To be sure we cannot fully understand the love that Christ has for the church. Scripture speaks of the breadth and length and height and depth of the love of Christ, which surpasses knowledge (**Ephesians. 3:17-19**).

Some Things We Do Know About Christ's Love For Us

---

1. **He loved us despite our sin (unconditionally) – Romans 5:8**
2. **He chose to love us (volitionally) – 1 John 4:10; Ephesians 1:4**
3. **His love is an intense love – John 13:1; Ephesians 5:2, 25**
4. **His love is an unending love – Jeremiah 31:3; Romans 8:38-39**
5. **His love is an unselfish love – Philippians 2:6-7**
6. **His love is a purposeful love – Ephesians 5:26-27;** He works for our improvement, our development, our happiness, our welfare.

7. **His love is a sacrificial love** – He loved us and gave himself for us. He died, the just for the unjust, to bring us to God. In love, He endured the horrible death of the cross with all of its physical and spiritual torture and agony. In love, He bore the guilt and penalty of sin and the wrath of God in the place of His people. In love, He personally bore our sins in His own body on the cross so that the penalty and power and devastating effects of sin in our lives might be broken **(Ephesians 5:2, 25; Galatians 2:20; I Peter 3:18; Romans 5:6-11; I Peter 2:24)**.

8. **His love is an obvious** (manifested) **love** – Christ manifests (shows) His love in words and deeds. He tells us He loves us. He shows us He loves us. He protects us, prays for us, guards us, strengthens us, helps us, defends us, teaches us, comforts us, chastens us, equips us, empathizes with us, and provides for all our needs **(John 10:1-14; 14:1-3; 13:34, 35; 15:9-10; Romans 8:32; Philippians 4:13, 19; Hebrews 4:14-16)**.

Since we are to love our wives like Christ loves the Church, (that is, as individual Christians) this then is the standard by which a husband is to judge his love for his wife!

1 Corinthians 13:4-7 is another very helpful passage. It goes to great lengths to describe **biblical actions of love...**

- **Suffereth long** – The Greek word is μακροθυμει (makrothumeo, mak-roth-oo-meh'-o; Strongs # 3114). It means to be long-spirited, patient, particularly with people as opposed to circumstances.

- **Kind** – The Greek word is χρηστευεμαι (chresteuomai, khraste-yoo'-om-ahee; 5541). It means to be kind, obliging, act benevolently, to be kind.

- **Envieth not** – The Greek word is ζηλοι (zeloo, dzay-lo'-o; 2206) which means to have warmth of feeling for or against or to be jealous over. It is in the negative form, so it is not to be done.

- **Vaunteth not itself** – The Greek word is περπερευεται (perpereuomai, per-per-yoo'-om-ahee; 4068) which means not to boast or brag. It is in the negative form, so it is not to be done.
- **Not puffed up** – The Greek word is φυσιουται (phusioo, foo-see-o'-o; 5448). It means to blow, to inflate or puff up. It is used figuratively here referring to someone who is conceited, self-centered and filled with pride. It is in the negative form, so it is not to be done.
- **Not unseemly** – The Greek word is ασχημονει (aschemoneo, as-kay-mon-eh'-o; 807) which means to act unbecoming or to behave in an ugly, indecent, unseemly, unbecoming manner, hence to be rude. It is in the negative form, so it is not to be done.
- **Seeketh not her own** – The Greek word behind seeketh is ζητει (zeteo, dzay-teh'-o; 2212). It means to worship, to plot, to strive for or to seek after. The Greek phrase "not her own" is the Greek word, εαυτης (heautou, heh-ow-too'; 1438) which means of himself, herself or itself. Therefore, love does not worship or focus on self but focuses on others.
- **Not easily provoked** – The Greek word is παροξυνεται (paroxuno, par-ox-oo'-no; 3947) which means to sharpen alongside, easily provoke, stir, irritate or exasperate. It is in the negative form, so it is not to be done.
- **Thinketh no evil** – The word "thinketh" is λογιζεται (logizomai, log-id'-zom-ahee; 3049). It means to take or keep an inventory. Therefore, love does not keep an inventory of evil.
- **Rejoiceth in truth** – The Greek word "rejoiceth" is χαιρει (chairo, khah'ee-ro; 5463) which means to be cheerful or calmly happy. The Greek word for "truth" is αληθεια (aletheia, al-ay'-thi-a; 225). It means what is true.

The indication is that love rejoices in conduct that conforms with the truth of God's word.

- **Beareth all things** – The Greek behind the English word "beareth" is στεγει (stego, steg'-o; 4722). It means to roof over or to cover with silence (endure patiently): forbear, suffer. In other words, love covers over or hides shortcomings and faults.
- **Believeth all things** – The Greek word is πιστευει (pisteuo, pist-yoo'-o; 4100) to have faith in, upon, or with respect to, a person or thing. In other words, true love trusts or has faith in the person that they love.
- **Hopeth all things** – The Greek word is ελπιζει (elpizo, el-pid'-zo;1679) to expect with desire, to hope. In other words, love desires the best for the one loved.
- **Endureth all things** – The Greek word is υπομενει (hupomeno, hoop-om-en'-o;5278). It means to stay under, remain, bear (trials), have fortitude, persevere: – abide, endure, (take) patient (-ly), suffer, tarry behind.

Men, when you measure your love for your wife by the 1 Corinthians 13 yardstick, how are you doing? Do you really love your wife as you love yourself? Are you really pressing toward the goal of loving your wife as Christ loved the church? Is your love for your wife unconditional, volitional, intensive, unending, unselfish, purposeful, sacrificial and obvious? **This is the kind of love that we are to have for our wives.**

✓Dr. Gill's Description of "Agapao"

The best description I have ever read of *Agapao* was written by the 18th century Baptist Preacher and theologian, Dr. John Gill. Read his characterization of *love* carefully as I have applied them to the wife.

- Agapao-love consists in a strong and cordial affection for your wife

- In taking a real delight and pleasure in her.

- In showing respect, and doing honour to them.

- In a quiet, constant, and comfortable dwelling with them.

- In providing all things necessary for them.

- In protecting them from all injuries and abuses.

- In concealing their faults, and covering their infirmities;

- In entertaining the best opinion of their persons and actions.

- In endeavoring to promote their spiritual good and welfare.

- This love ought to be hearty and sincere, and not feigned and selfish.

- It should be shown in private, as well as in public.It should be chaste and single, constant and perpetual.

- It should exceed that which is shown to neighbors, or even to parents.

- It should be at least equal to that which a man shows to himself.

Tangible Ways You Can Love Your Wife

- **Listen to her and talk to her while giving her your full attention** (Proverbs 25:11)

- **Provide for her needs** (1 Timothy 5:8; Ephesians 5:28) – Physical, emotional, social, intellectual, sexual, spiritual needs

- **Protect her** (Ephesians 5:29; 1 Peter 3:7) ...from trying to do more then she can or should do ...and give her a breather from the demands of the children

- **Help her** (Ephesians 5:25)

- **Encourage her** (Ephesians 4:29)

- **Sacrifice for her, choose to do her will** (Ephesians 5:25)

- **Share your life with her and encourage her to share hers with you** (1 Peter 3:7)

- **Be satisfied with her** (Proverbs 5:19)

- **Make her first place** (1 Peter 3:7)

- **Express commitment to her** (Matthew 19:6)

- **Treat her tenderly, courteously, respectfully** (Ephesians 4:32)

- **Overlook her faults** (1 Peter 4:8; Colossians 3:13)

- **Openly show that you cherish and appreciate her** (Ephesians 5:29, 2 Timothy 3:2 – not unthankful)

God's Will For Every Husband Is That He Love His Wife!

Now on to the second point...

---

2) A HUSBAND IS RESPONSIBLE TO LEAD HIS WIFE

Genesis 3:16 *Unto the woman he said, I will greatly multiply thy sorrow and thy conception; in sorrow thou shalt bring forth children; and thy desire shall be to thy husband, and he shall rule over thee.*

Ephesians 5:23 *For the husband is the head of the wife, even as Christ is the head of the church: and he is the saviour of the body.*

1 Corinthians 11:3 *But I would have you know, that the head of every man is Christ; and the head of the woman is the man; and the head of Christ is God.*

1 Timothy 3:4-5 *One that ruleth well his own house, having his children in subjection with all gravity; 5 (For if a man know not how to rule his own house, how shall he take care of the church of God?)*

1 Timothy 2:11-14 *Let the woman learn in silence with all subjection. 12 But I suffer not a woman to teach, nor to usurp authority over the man, but to be in silence. 13 For Adam was first formed, then Eve. 14 And Adam was not* *deceived, but the woman being deceived was in the transgression.*

The Bible is clear. The husband has the God ordained responsibility to be the head of his wife and the head of the home. He will be accountable to God for how he exercises that leadership!

Now, since men have that responsibility and will be held responsible for how we lead our wives and our homes, we need to understand what headship or leadership really is!

WHAT IS SOCIETY'S CONCEPT OF LEADERSHIP?

(North Korean Dictator Kim Jong-un) Many think of a leader as <u>one who barks out orders</u> and <u>bosses others around</u>. Others hold the dictatorial view of leadership looking at leadership as empowering the leader with absolute power and supreme authority. Others look at leadership as one who guides the group.

The **dictionary definition** of a leader is this… "A person or thing that leads; directing, commanding, or guiding head, as of a group or activity."

Then the dictionary gives several illustrations of leadership:

Music: The conductor is a leader; the main performer in an instrumental or vocal section is a leader.

Horses: A lead horse is first in the harness before all others in the same hitch.

I believe that the best example of a husband's leadership is the lead horse. He should be the first in the harness and the first to pull, leading the way for all the rest of the family.

THE BIBLICAL DESIGN OF LEADERSHIP

Matthew 20:20-28 reveals Christ's Design of Leadership. It shows us what leadership is and what it is not.

Matthew 20:20-28 *Then came to him the mother of Zebedee's children with her sons, worshipping him, and desiring a certain thing of him. 21 And he said unto her, What wilt thou? She saith unto him, Grant that these my two sons* *may sit, the one on thy right hand, and the other on the left, in thy kingdom. 22 But Jesus answered and said, Ye know not what ye ask. Are ye able to drink of the cup that I shall drink of, and to be baptized with the baptism that I am baptized with? They say unto him, We are able. 23 And he saith unto them, Ye shall drink indeed of my cup, and be baptized with the baptism that I am baptized with: but to sit on my right hand, and on my left, is not mine to give, but it shall be given to them for whom it is prepared of my Father. 24 And when the ten heard it, they were moved with indignation against the two brethren. 25 But Jesus called them unto him, and said, Ye know that the princes of the Gentiles exercise* **dominion over them** (2634 – katakurieuo, kat-ak-oo-ree-yoo'-o; to lord against, i.e. control, subjugate*), and they that are great exercise authority upon them* (2715 – katexousiazo, kat-ex-oo-see-ad'-zo; to have (wield) full privilege over: domineer*). 26 But* **it shall not be so among you***: but whosoever will be great among you, let him be your* **minister** (1249. diakonos, dee-ak'-on-os – to run on errands; a waiter)*; 27 And whosoever will be chief among you, let him be your* **servant** (1401. doulos, doo'-los – a servant, a slave; one who is in a permanent relationship of servitude to another)*: 28 Even as the Son of man came* <u>*not*</u> *to be* **ministered unto** (1247. diakoneo, dee-ak-on-eh'-o; – to be an attendant, i.e. wait upon)*, but to* **minister** (1247)*, and to give his life a ransom for many.*

This passage gives us the Bible's concept of a leader. According to this passage, **a true leader is first and foremost a servant**. His concern is <u>not</u> for himself or having his own way but the main concern of a leader is to meet the needs of others. Indeed, if <u>the best interests of others</u> are not on his heart, he is not a biblical leader. When I refer to the "best interest of others" I am not referring to helping others do or get what they want, but helping them to do or get what they need. And this is within a biblical context. For instance, a father will train up his children in the way they should go, not the way they want to go

(Prov. 22:6). This is in the child's best interest. This is biblical leadership.

John 13:1-15 gives us the same picture of what it means to be a leader. In this passage, the emblem of leadership is not a throne or a club but a big towel and a basin. In other words, a leader must have a servant's heart. And if he has a servant's heart, he will <u>act like a servant</u> and <u>react like a servant</u>. Like a lead horse, he is first in the harness and leads by example. Therefore, a husband is to be the chief servant, first in the harness, pulling his load and helping the others to pull their loads.

More Examples of New Testament Leadership

Pastors and Church Leaders -- 1 Peter 5:3 *Neither as being lords over God's heritage, but being <u>ensamples</u> to the flock.* The word *"lords"* is the Greek word (katakurieuo - kat-ak-oo-ree-yoo'-o; 2634) which means to lord against or to control, subjugate. *"Ensamples"* is the Greek word tupos (too'-pos - 5179) which means a model or pattern. In the context, pastors and church leaders are to be models or patterns of Christ. Therefore, a husband is to be a model or pattern of Christ in his home!

1 Thessalonians 2:5-11 *For neither at any time used we flattering words, as ye know, nor a cloak of covetousness; God is witness: 6 Nor of men sought we glory, neither of you, nor yet of others, when we might have been burdensome, as the apostles of Christ. 7 But we were gentle among you, even as a nurse cherisheth her children: 8 So being affectionately desirous of you, we were willing to have <u>imparted unto you, not the gospel of God only, but also our own souls</u>, because ye were dear unto us. 9 For ye remember, brethren, our labour and travail: for labouring night and day, because we would not be chargeable unto any of you, we preached unto you the* *gospel of God. 10 Ye are witnesses, and God also, how holily and justly and unblameably we behaved ourselves among you that believe: 11 As ye know how we exhorted and comforted and charged every one of you, as a father doth his children.*

The Biblical Concept of Leadership Applied to the Husband –

Being a leader, biblically speaking, means that the husband must be the family's biggest servant. He leads by example. He is **not a cruel dictator,** but a loving leader, with the best interests of his wife on his heart, leading by example. (**Colossians 3:19**)

Men, we need to measure our headship by the following passage...

Ephesians 5:23-29 *For the husband is the head of the wife, even as Christ is the head of the church: and he is the saviour of the body. 24 Therefore as the church is subject unto Christ, so let the wives be to their own husbands in every thing. 25 Husbands, love your wives, even as Christ also loved the church, and gave himself for it; 26 That he might sanctify and cleanse it with the washing of water by the word, 27 That he might present it to himself a glorious church, not having spot, or wrinkle, or any such thing; but that it should be holy and without blemish. 28 So ought men to love their wives as their own bodies. He that loveth his wife loveth himself. 29 For no man ever yet hated his own flesh; but nourisheth and cherisheth it, even as the Lord the church:*

What do we see about the husband's headship in this passage?

First, he is to be the head of his wife *even as* Christ is the head of the church. **What does that mean?**

Men, our great model in leadership is Jesus Christ, who made Himself a servant (**Phil. 2:6-8**); who came not to be served, but to serve, and to give His life a ransom for many (**Mark 10:45**); who is head over all things for the sake of the church (**Eph. 1:22, 23**). Whatever Jesus Christ does, He does for our sake, He does with our best interests at heart.

In similar fashion, the husband is to have his wife's best interests at heart as indicated by **1 Peter 3:7**.

God's Will For Every Husband Is That He Be A Servant-Leader Not A Cruel Dictator.

Christ's Example of Leadership
Specific Ways Jesus Christ Led His Disciples

Jesus Christ is to be our great leadership model. Therefore, we can learn a great deal about how we are to lead our wife and family by examining how he lead his disciples.

• **Jesus Christ practiced the principle of continuous association with those whom He led.**

For over three years, He **spent great amounts of time with them**. (Compare John 1:39, 43; Mark 1:17; 3:14; 4:10; 5:1, 30, 31, 39-40; 6:1,30,31,32,35; 8:1,10,27,34; 9:2,30; 10:13,23, 46; 11:1.) **Biblical leadership requires association with those who are being led.**

Application to Marriage – *1 Peter 3:7 Likewise, ye husbands, dwell* (together with) *with them according to knowledge, giving honour unto the wife, as unto the weaker vessel, and as being heirs together of the grace of life; that your prayers be not hindered.*

We are to spend time with our wife. We are to get to know what makes them **tick** and what makes them **ticked**. No husband is fulfilling his God-given responsibility to his wife who does not delight in and arrange for frequent and regular companionship with her.

- **Jesus Christ carefully and relevantly taught His disciples**

    In many places, Scripture asserts that <u>Jesus taught His disciples</u>. (Compare Matt. 5:1-2; Mark 4:10; John 13-16.) In fact, the word *"teacher"* was one of the titles by which Jesus was frequently called (John 3: 2; 13: 13).

    How did Christ teach his disciples? Sometimes He taught His disciples in a <u>formal way</u> (Matthew 5: 1, 2; John 13-16). On other occasions He taught them in an <u>informal way,</u> in the midst of life situations, when He was faced by a crisis or confrontation, or when He was asked a question (Matthew 19:3-12, 16-27; 21: 12-32). But whether He taught them in a formal or informal way, it is an established fact that Jesus Christ led and served His disciples by teaching them.

    Application to Marriage – God also expects the husband to lead his wife by **teaching her**. Wives, are you teachable?

    1 Corinthians 14:35 *And if they will learn any thing, let them <u>ask their husbands at home</u>: for it is a shame for women to speak in the church.*

    Ephesians 5:25-26 *Husbands, love your wives, even as Christ also loved the church, and gave himself for it; 26 That he might sanctify and cleanse it with the washing of water by the word.*

- **Jesus Christ led His disciples by being a good example.**

Frequently as we read the Gospels, we hear Jesus saying, *"Follow me,"* (Matthew 4:19) or *"Come after me,"* (Mark 8:34) or *"I have given you an example."* (John 13:15). He did not simply tell men that they ought always to pray, he lived a life of constant prayer. He did not merely preach to men that the Scriptures should be their final authority. He lived a life, which was an example of what it means to make the Scriptures the final authority in your life. His life then was an example in living color of what He wanted His disciples to believe and how He wanted them to live. On the one hand, His exemplary life was a pattern or model for His disciples to follow. On the other hand, it earned their respect and made them willing to submit to His authority and leadership. The disciples followed this same pattern and encouraged New Testament believers to do the same.

Philippians 4:9 *Those things, which ye have both learned, and received, and heard, and seen in me, do: and the God of peace shall be with you.*

1 Peter 5:3 *Neither as being lords over God's heritage, but being ensamples to the flock.*

Application to Marriage – As husband-leaders, we must strive to be an example, a model, a pattern of godliness, holiness, compassion, dedication, and devotion to God. To be sure, we still have our sin natures and no husband will ever be a perfect example for his wife, but that is what we should strive for. **Philippians 3:12-14** says, *Not as though I had already attained, either were already perfect: but I follow after, if that I may apprehend that for which also I am apprehended of Christ Jesus. 13 Brethren, I count not myself to have apprehended: but this one thing I do, forgetting those things which are* *behind, and reaching forth unto those things which are before, 14 I press toward the mark for the prize of the high calling of God in Christ Jesus.*

When we fail, we should be quick to confess to God and our wife that we have failed and ask for forgiveness. Even in failure, the husband must be an example to his wife of how the believer should deal with sin. In failure, as well as at all other times, the Christian husband is to lead his wife by the power and authority of a good example.

- **Jesus Christ led His disciples by making decisions and delegating responsibility to them**

   John 4:1-2 *When therefore the Lord knew how the Pharisees had heard that Jesus made and baptized more disciples than John, 2 (Though Jesus himself baptized not, but his disciples,)*

   Matthew 21:1-6 This passage makes it obvious that Jesus made decisions and delegated responsibilities to His disciples. Note that when Jesus delegated, He gave clear, concise, and specific directions so that the disciples knew what was expected of them and how they should go about their tasks. He also took into consideration their fears, needs, questions, spiritual, emotional, and physical state (See **John 11:20-40**). He gave them a basic framework in which to work but he also gave them freedom within that framework.

   Application to Marriage – Christian husbands are called upon to lead their wives by making decisions and by delegating responsibility. To be the leader does not mean that he must bear all the responsibility and do all the work while his wife bears nothing and does nothing. It does mean that he will see to it that the work gets done and that everyone knows who does what. Husbands are supposed to lead, and leading involves making decisions and delegating responsibility. **NOTE:** Any organization where only two people are involved needs someone who is final authority, or chaos and confusion will result. <u>Fifty-fifty marriages are an impossibility</u>. They do not work. They cannot work. **In marriage someone has to be the final decision maker.** Someone has to delegate responsibility, and **God has ordained that this should be the husband.** Her opinions, advice, desires, suggestions, requests, fears, and questions should be given serious consideration. The wife is to be the husband's <u>helper</u>. She is to be his <u>chief adviser</u>, <u>resource person</u>, and <u>consultant</u>. He may decide to allow his wife to make decisions (e.g., where they will go on vacation, what rugs or drapes or furniture they will buy), but **he must never relinquish his overall decision-making responsibility.** God has called the husband to be his wife's leader, and he <u>cannot</u> be her leader by being her follower.

In summary, of the many elements involved in developing genuine oneness, none is more important than leadership. If genuine oneness is to be experienced, the lifestyle of the wife must be genuine biblical submission. Conversely, the lifestyle of the husband must be the kind of leadership that has just been described.

> ## God's Will For Every Husband Is That He Lead His Wife! Are You Being A Loving Leader?

[Much of the above material was adapted from *Strengthening Your Marriage* by Wayne Mack]

CHAPTER 3
GOD'S BLUEPRINT FOR WIVES

In the early years of my marriage, we purchased and assembled our own storage cabinet from Sears. When I got it home I tore open the box, laid out the pieces on the floor and began to assemble the cabinet. My dear wife sweetly said, "don't you think you should look at the directions first?" I responded something to the effect, "No, it looks like a piece of cake." After all I had a toolbox filled with Craftsman tools and I had worked in a machine shop.

Well, I have to tell you that I got that cabinet 80% done. I was so proud of my self! I was just a hair breath from gloating. And then I came to the realization that try as I might, I could not get the main shelf into the cabinet. I tried everything. I pulled. I stuck my tongue out. I grunted and tried to force it into place. What was I going to do? It just would not fit. But the worst part for me was that I, a gifted and talented new husband with mechanical ability, was going to have to "eat crow" and admit to my wife that...SHE WAS RIGHT! I should have looked at the directions first!

I swallowed hard, forced a smile and said, "I guess I am going to have to take a look at those directions. I can't figure out how to get this stupid shelf in."

That was my wife's golden opportunity. She could have said, "I told you so." But, she resisted the temptation and offered to read the directions to me. As it turned out, I had to tear the cabinet apart and go back to nearly the first step. Today, every time I go down to the family room I see that cabinet. It stands as a reminder to me that it is important to *follow the instructions*.

The truth is that many marriages are in trouble today because the couple goes about their marriage just like I was going about trying to put the cabinet together. They figure that they are intelligent people and besides they love each other so they try to put their marriage together the way they think it should fit. But, they soon find out that it is not fitting together like it should. Confusion, and frustration set in and before you know it all the joy is gone. So what should you do? **God has provided specific instructions on how a marriage is to work**! God has revealed specific information and direction concerning the purpose of marriage and the varying but complementary responsibilities of the two people who form the marriage. God has given certain responsibilities to the wife and certain responsibilities to the husband. *When two people know, accept, and fulfill their varying but complementary responsibilities, oneness in marriage is promoted.* But, when the husband and wife either do not understand or will not fulfill their God-given responsibilities, great confusion and frustration is the result. What I am saying is **follow the instructions God has given!**

We have previously considered the husband's responsibility to his wife; 1) **He is to love his wife** 2) **He is to lead his wife**. This is God's will for each husband. In this chapter, we are going to focus on the wife's responsibility to her husband.

A Wife's Two Key Responsibilities To Her Husband

1. She is to submit to her husband
2. She is to assist, aid and complete her husband

Let's focus on the first point...

1)   A Wife Is Responsible To Submit To Her Husband

While the idea of the wife's submission to her husband is not a very popular one in our day, it is God's will that a wife submits to her husband. The woman's liberation movement has gone to great lengths to undermine the Biblical truths of the role of the wife in marriage. There is a great deal of antagonism to wifely submission that has arisen even in Christian circles because many Christian women have adopted the rebellious attitudes and accepted the teachings of the modern woman's movement concerning their role in the home. To follow the world in this matter is nothing less than rebellion against God. Today's family problems stem from husbands and wives who refuse to follow God's instructions.

✓ **Word Studies Related To Submission**

The key passage that deals with submission is...

Ephesians 5:22-24 & 33 *Wives, submit yourselves unto your own husbands, as unto the Lord. 23 For the husband is the head of the wife, even as Christ is the head of the church: and he is the saviour of the body. 24 **Therefore as the church is subject unto Christ, so let the wives be to their own***

husbands in every thing. 33 Nevertheless let every one of you in particular so love his wife even as himself; and the wife see that she <u>reverence</u> her husband.

The Greek word translated **submit** in verse 22 & **subject** in verse 24 is from the word υποτασσεσθε (hoop-ot-as'-so; 5293). It means 1) to arrange under, to subordinate 2) to subject, put in subjection 3) to subject one's self, obey 4) to submit to one's control 5) to yield to one's admonition or advice 6) to obey, be subject. The word is a Greek military term meaning "to arrange *troop divisions* in a military fashion under the command of a leader". In non-military use, it was "a voluntary attitude of giving in, cooperating, assuming responsibility, and carrying a burden".

That brings me to the word **reverence** in **verse 33**. It is the Greek word φοβηται (fob-eh'-o; 5399) to fear; to be afraid; to treat with deference or reverential obedience.

It is interesting to see how Bible translators have translated this verse –

- **1380 Wycliff**
  "…the wife dread her husband."
- **1534 Tyndale**
  "…And let the wife see that she fear her husband."
- **1557 Geneva Bible**
  "…let the wife see that she fear her husband."
- **16ll King James Version**
  "…the wife see that she reverence her husband."

Now, I know someone is thinking, "Pastor, are you saying that a wife should be 'afraid' of her husband?" Let me make myself clear. A wife should continually treat her husband with deference and reverential obedience. Indeed, she should be fearful not to submit to him for **as the church is subject unto Christ, so let the wives be to their own husbands in every** *thing*. (24). Simply stated, every wife will give account to Christ as to how she submitted to her husband. That is why she should be afraid not to obey her husband.

Other Related Verses

Colossians 3:18 *Wives, submit (5293) yourselves unto your own husbands, as it is fit* (proper) *in the Lord.*

Titus 2:4-5 *That they may teach the young women to be sober, to love their husbands, to love their children, 5 To be discreet, chaste, keepers at home, good, obedient (5293) to their own husbands, that the word of God be not blasphemed.*

1 Peter 3:1-6 *Likewise, ye wives, be in subjection (5293) to your own husbands; that, if any obey not the word, they also may without the word be won by the conversation of the wives; 2 While they behold your chaste conversation coupled with fear* (5401, same root as 5399). *3 Whose adorning let it not be that outward adorning of plaiting the hair, and of wearing of gold, or of putting on of apparel; 4 But let it be the hidden man of the heart, in that which is not corruptible, even the ornament of a meek and quiet spirit, which is in the sight of God of great price. 5 For after this manner in the old time the holy women also, who trusted in God, adorned themselves, being in subjection (5293) unto their own husbands: 6 Even as Sara obeyed Abraham, calling him lord: whose daughters ye are, as long as ye do well, and are not afraid with any amazement.*

A Christian wife cannot be a Godly wife if she does not submit to her husband. But, what do you do if your husband is unsaved or if your husband is a Christian but out of fellowship with God? The answer is the same. You submit to your husband. In fact, in the above verse there is a special promise to those who submit to ungodly or rebellious husbands.

Dr. Warren Wiersbe says this about **verse 6**.

Peter closed this section by pointing to Sarah as an example of a godly, submissive wife. Christian wives today would probably embarrass their husbands if they called them "lord," but their attitudes ought to be such that they could call them "lord" and people would believe it. The believing wife who submits to Christ and to her husband, and who cultivates a "meek and quiet spirit" will never have to be afraid. The "fear" in this verse means "terror"...God will watch over her even when her unsaved mate creates problems and difficulties for her.

Henry Alford comments in his Commentary on the New Testament, *"As long as the believing wives are doing good, they need not be afraid with any sudden terror of the account which unbelieving husbands may exact from them."*

I do however want to point out this important fact. If a husband would direct the wife to do something that the Bible forbids, such things as murdering, stealing, participating in sexual activity outside the marriage bond, etc., then **Acts 5:29** comes into play – *Then Peter and the other apostles answered and said, We ought to obey God rather than men.*

> **God's Will For Every Wife Is That She Submit To Her Husband!**

WHAT SUBMISSION DOES NOT MEAN

- **Submission Does Not Mean The Wife Becomes A Slave**

The definition of a slave is, "a human being who is owned by and absolutely subject to another human being, as by capture, purchase, or birth." A husband does not own his wife! She is not his possession. She is his companion, completer, compliment, helper and assistant. The Bible never describes a wife as a slave but rather one that the husband is to be joined or cleave to. **Ephesians 5:31** *For this cause shall a man leave his father and mother, and shall be joined unto his wife, and they two shall be one flesh.* (Mat. 19:5 - cleave). Any husband who treats his wife as "his property" or as a slave is in trouble with God! That is NOT how a wife is to be treated. Husbands, we are to cherish our wives!

In reality, submission frees the wife to function within the parameters of the husband's direction. Submission frees the wife to become all that God intends her to become.

- **Submission Does Not Mean The Wife Is Inferior To The Husband**

Let me ask you a question. "Was Jesus Christ inferior to Mary and Joseph?" The answer to that is most certainly "NO!" But, turn to **Luke 2:51** *And he went down with them, and came to Nazareth, and <u>was subject unto them</u>: but his mother kept all these sayings in her heart.* Though Christ was not inferior to Mary and Joseph, he submitted to them. But there is more. Christ also submitted to his Heavenly Father and yet Jesus Christ was in no way inferior to God the Father. He was and is fully and completely God, in every sense (Colossians 2:9). Yet the Scripture asserts that there is order and structure in the Trinity. Jesus said, *I can of mine own self do nothing: as I hear, I judge: and my judgment is just; because I seek not mine own will, but the will of the Father which hath sent me.* **John 5:30**. The apostle Paul declared in **1 Corinthians 11:3** *But I would have you know, that the head of every man is Christ; and the head of the woman is the man; and the head of Christ is God.* Again, this certainly does not imply that Christ is inferior to God the Father. Rather it teaches that there is a division of labor and responsibility in the Trinity. In like fashion, the submission of the wife in no way implies inferiority. Instead, it teaches the necessity for order and structure, for a division of responsibility within the home. God has chosen the husband to be the loving leader in the home. He has chosen the wife to be in the support role in the home, not the slave. In fact, I also turn your attention to the fact that husbands are to honor their wives! *Honor* means to consider very valuable or precious. **1 Peter 3:7** *Likewise, ye husbands, dwell with them according to knowledge, giving honour unto the wife, as unto the weaker vessel, and as being heirs together of the grace of life; that your prayers be not hindered.*

One additional thought before I move on. When it comes to your spiritual relationship with God there is no division of responsibility, men and women are equal. **Galatians 3:28** *There is neither Jew nor Greek, there is neither bond nor free, there is neither male nor female: for ye are all one in Christ Jesus.* The ground is level at the Cross!

- **Submission Does Not Mean The Wife Never Opens Her Mouth, Never Has An Opinion or Never Gives Advice.**

Some people have mistakenly interpreted **1 Peter 3:4** *"...the ornament of a meek and quiet spirit..."* to say that a woman is to keep her mouth shut and may not express her opinion or offer advice in the context of the family relationship. While women are to be silent in the preaching and teaching roles over men in the church, though they may teach children (1 Timothy 2:11-14), this does not apply to the home. When a wife expresses herself in the home it is to be with a *meek and quiet spirit.* The word **meek** is the Greek word πραεος (prah-ooce' 4239) which means mild or gentle. The word **quiet** is the translation of the Greek word ησυχιου (hay-soo'-khee-os; 2272) which means to keep your seat, to be tranquil, peaceful or undisturbed by outward circumstances. Therefore, this is not an injunction to keep silent, rather, when she does express herself it is in a gentle, tranquil way not in a bold, assertive, brassy, loud way. In fact, **Proverbs 15:1** wonderfully contrasts the right way and the wrong way for a wife (or anyone) to express herself – *A soft answer turneth away wrath: but grievous words stir up anger.* There is an additional verse I want to point out before I go on. **Proverbs 31:26** *She openeth her mouth with wisdom; and in her tongue is the law of kindness.* Indeed, a wife will offer advice properly and a wise husband will listen and carefully weigh what she has to say.

- **Submission Does Not Mean The Wife Becomes A Wallflower Who Never Uses Her Gifts & Abilities**

Proverbs 31:10-31 is God's example of a Biblical wife. Even a quick reading shows that this woman made full use of the talents and abilities God gave her.

WHAT SUBMISSION DOES MEAN

- **Scripture indicates that it is the wife's responsibility to make herself submissive**

Nowhere is the husband commanded to physically force his wife into submission. Rather, the **wife is commanded to make** herself submissive.
(See **Ephesians 5:22** & **1 Peter 3:1**)

- **Scripture indicates that the wife's submission is to be continuous**

The Greek verb in most passages about submission is in the present tense. Therefore, submission is to be the continuous life style of the wife. (See **Ephesians 5:22** & **1 Peter 3:1**)

- **Wifely submission is mandatory, not optional**

The Greek verb is in the imperative mood. (Compare **Ephesians 5:21, 22** and **I Peter 3:1**) Her submission is not to be based upon the way her husband treats her. Nor is it to be conditioned by the husband's abilities, talents, wisdom, education, or spiritual state. (**I Peter 3:1**)

- **Wifely submission is a spiritual matter, done "as to the Lord"**

Ephesians 5:22 *Wives, submit yourselves unto your own husbands, as unto the Lord.* Refusal to submit to the husband is therefore rebellion against God Himself. Submission to the husband is a test of her love for God as well as a test of love for her husband. The wife then must look upon her submission to her husband as an act of obedience to Christ and not merely to her husband. Jesus said, *If ye love me, keep my commandments.* (John 14:15), and one of his commands to wives is, *"submit yourselves unto your own husbands..."*

- **Submission is a positive, not negative concept**

It emphasizes what the wife should do, rather than what she should not do. Submission means that the wife puts all of her talents, abilities, resources, energy at her husband's disposal. Submission means that the wife yields and uses all of her abilities under the management of her husband for the good of her husband and family. Submission means that she sees herself as a part of her husband's team. She is not her husband's opponent fighting at cross purposes or trying to outdo him. She is not merely an individual going her separate way. She is her husband's teammate striving for the same goal. She has ideas, opinions, desires, requests, and insights, and she lovingly makes them known. But she knows that on any good team, someone has to make the final decisions and plans. She knows that the team members must support the team leader, his plans and decisions, or no progress will be made, and confusion and frustration will result.

- **Submission involves the wife's attitudes as well as her actions**

Jesus Christ was thoroughly submitted to the Father. *Jesus saith unto them, My meat is to do the will of him that sent me, and to finish his work.* (John 4:34). But how did He serve the Father? He served the Father with gladness. He delighted to do the Father's will (**Psalm 40:7, 8**). Likewise, the wife's submission to her husband is to be cheerful, not servile or grudging. Scripture declares that God's kind of wife *worketh willingly with her hands.* (Prov. 31:13), finding great satisfaction in using all of her God-given resources to fulfill the needs of her husband and family.

- **Wifely submission is to be extensive**

She is to be subject unto her husband *as* the church is to Christ (Eph. 5:24). And how broad should the submission of the church be to Christ? Well, the submission of the church to Christ is to be total; it is to be comprehensive. Christ is *the head over all things to the church,* (Eph. 1:22), and the church is to do whatever it does in word or deed in the name of the Lord Jesus, in total dependence upon His person, acknowledging and recognizing Him in all its ways, doing all for His honor and glory (Col. 3:17; Prov. 3:5, 6; I Cor. 10:31). In like fashion Paul says, wives are to be subject to their husbands in *"every thing."* Submission is not to be an on-again off-again matter for the wife. Nor is it to be a selective, choose what you like, reject what you do not like proposition. Submission is to be her life style at all times, in all places, and in everything. Certainly this does not mean that she must obey her husband when he commands her to do what God forbids or tries to keep her from doing what God commands. She is to be subject to her husband *"as is fitting in the Lord"* (Col. 3:18). A wife's submission to her husband then is to be extensive, but not necessarily total or unlimited. She is to obey him in everything except that which contradicts the Word of God. And even then she is to disobey in a loving, submissive fashion, explaining calmly and clearly her reasons for disobedience, assuring her husband of her love and loyalty, and seeking to demonstrate that love and loyalty in a variety of continuous and tangible ways. She is to be her husband's helper (Gen. 2:18), and this she can never be if she manifests a contentious, inconsiderate, uncooperative spirit.

> **God's Will For Every Wife Is That She Submit To Her Husband & Reverence Him!**

Tangible Ways You Can Reverence Your Husband

- **Make it obvious to others and your children that your husband "wears the pants" in the family** (Ephesians 5:23)
- **Do not speak to your husband sarcastically or in a condescending manner** (Proverbs 21:19)
- **Don't contradict him in front of others** (Proverbs 31:12)
- **Don't talk for your husband or interrupt him when he is speaking** (1 Corinthians 13:4-5)
- **Treat your husband in private as respectfully as you do your pastor, neighbor, or friend in public** (1 Peter 2:17)
- **Do not bring up his shortcomings to others** (Proverbs 31:23)
- **Do not compare your husband unfavorably with other men** (Philippians 4:11)
- **Listen to his opinion carefully and try to understand him** (James 1:19)
- **Respect his requests by trying to do as he asks, even if it does not seem important to you** (Ephesians 5:24)

- **Respect his position in the home so that he can depend on you to do as he asks even when he is not there** (Proverbs 31:11)
- **Do not nag, pester or quarrel with him about things you want done, but tactfully appeal to him** (Proverbs 27:15)
- **Rearrange your schedule so that you are available to spend time with him and meet his needs** (Titus 2:4)
- **Do not try to manipulate or bully him by making a threat, whining, crying or withholding marital privileges** (Proverbs 25:24; 1 Corinthians 7:4-7)
- **Praise him for his good character qualities** (Proverbs 14:1)
- **Admit it when you are wrong** (James 5:16)
- **Show a grateful spirit by letting him know you appreciate him and the things he provides** (Colossians 3:15)

God's Will For Every Wife Is That She Reverence Her Husband!

Let's move on to the **Wife's Second Key Responsibility To Her Husband...**

---

2) A Wife Is Responsible To Help, Assist, Aid And Complete Her Husband

An honest examination of the Scriptures leads to the conclusion that the wife's primary ministry in life is her husband. The first indication we have of this is found in **Genesis 2:18-22**. This passage reveals several important details about the wife's relationship to her husband.

God made the woman to be man's helper.

It is important for men to see that without the woman, man, even in his perfect condition, was incomplete.

God made the woman to be a <u>suitable</u> helper.

None of the animals could provide the kind of help that man needed. Only woman could do that. **Proverbs 18:22**

Whoso findeth a wife findeth a good thing, and obtaineth favour of the LORD. **Proverbs 31:10-11** *Who can find a virtuous woman? for her price is far above rubies. 11 The heart of her husband doth safely trust in her, so that he shall have no need of spoil.*

God created the woman to correspond to man. She is similar to man, yet somewhat different. She is man's complement, not his carbon copy. She is to man what a key is to a lock and what a film is to a camera – indispensable. **1 Corinthians 11:11** *Nevertheless neither is the man without the woman, neither the woman without the man, in the Lord.*

It is clear from the Bible, that the wife was made to fulfill the needs, the lacks, and the inadequacies of her husband. She was made to be *her husband's unique helper.* She is to "do him good and not evil all the days of her life" (**Proverbs 31:12**). She is to be like a *fruitful vine* in her husband's house (**Psalm 128:3**). She is to be "*one flesh*" with her husband, and this will happen only as she accepts and fulfills her God-appointed role in marriage.

This does not mean that everything she does must have a direct connection to her husband. Nor does it mean that she should never do anything for her own benefit or for the benefit of others, or that she should never become involved in activities or ministries outside the home. But, ***it does mean, however, that she ought never to do anything which would be detrimental or harmful to her husband*** or that would cause her to neglect her primary ministry of helping her husband (Prov. 31: 10-31).

| **Some Ways A Wife Can Fulfill Her Role As Her Husband's Helper** |

- **Be affectionate to your husband**

Titus 2:4 *That they may teach the young women to be sober,* <u>*to love their husbands,*</u> *to love their children.* The word *love* in this verse is φιλανδρους (fil'-an-dros 5362) which means to be affectionate to your husband, to be your husband's affectionate companion.

- **Make your home a place of comfort and refuge**

Titus 2:5 *To be discreet, chaste,* <u>*keepers at home,*</u> *good, obedient to their own husbands, that the word of God be not blasphemed.*

The main focus of a wife is not to be her career, but her husband, home and children. The home should be a place of comfort and refuge. Avoid the danger of allowing the home to be in shambles and full of disorder and confusion. But also avoid the danger of making the house a show place where everything must always be neat and immaculate. Most husbands want homes to live in, not a show place to visit.

- **Be trustworthy and dependable**

Proverbs 31:11-12 *The heart of her husband doth safely trust in her, so that he shall have no need of spoil. 12 She will do him good and not evil all the days of her life.*

- **Cooperate with your husband in raising children and keeping the household running**

Proverbs 31:26-28 *She openeth her mouth with wisdom; and in her tongue is the law of kindness. 27 She looketh well to the ways of her household, and eateth not the bread of idleness. 28 Her children arise up, and call her blessed; her husband also, and he praiseth her.*

Titus 2:4 *That they may teach the young women to... love their children.* The word *"love"* means to be fond of, therefore to be fond of your children or maternal.

1 Timothy 5:13-14 *And withal they learn to be idle, wandering about from house to house; and not only idle, but tattlers also and busybodies, speaking things which they ought not. 14 I will therefore that the younger women marry, bear children, guide the house, give none occasion to the adversary to speak reproachfully.* The phrase *"guide the house"* is but one Greek word, οικοδεσποτειν (oikodespoteo, oy-kod-es-pot-eh'-o; 3616) which means one who manages domestic affairs or the home.

- **Be an industrious, frugal, diligent, ambitious, and creative member of the team – Proverbs 10:13-24**

- **Being satisfied with your position, your possessions, and your tasks**

Philippians 4:6-13 *Be careful for nothing; but in every thing by prayer and supplication with thanksgiving let your requests be made known unto God. 7 And the peace of God, which passeth all understanding, shall keep your hearts and minds through Christ Jesus. 8 Finally, brethren, whatsoever things are true, whatsoever things are honest, whatsoever things are just, whatsoever things are pure, whatsoever things are lovely, whatsoever things are of good report; if there be any virtue, and if there be any praise, think on these things. 9 Those things, which ye have both learned, and received, and heard, and seen in me, do: and the God of peace shall be with you. 10 But I rejoiced in the Lord greatly, that now at the last your care of me hath flourished again; wherein ye were also careful, but ye lacked opportunity. 11 Not that I speak in respect of want: for I have learned, in whatsoever state I am, therewith to be content. 12 I know both how to be abased, and I know how to abound: every where and in all things I am instructed both to be full and to be* *hungry, both to abound and to suffer need. 13 I can do all things through Christ which strengtheneth me.*

Hebrews 13:5 *Let your conversation be without covetousness; and be content with such things as ye have: for he hath said, I will never leave thee, nor forsake thee.*

- **Offer suggestions and advice and discuss things openly and honestly in a loving fashion**

  Proverbs 31:26 *She openeth her mouth with wisdom; and in her tongue is the law of kindness.*
  Ephesians 4:25 *Wherefore putting away lying, speak every man truth with his neighbour: for we are members one of another.*

God's Will For Every Wife Is That She Help Her Husband. Are You Your Husband's Helper?

CHAPTER 4
GOD'S BLUEPRINT FOR COMMUNICATION

Communication is important! And good communication is especially important if there is to be unity in any undertaking, especially marriage. Let us focus on communication.

Outline

- **The Definition of Communication**
- **Three Main Types of Communication**
    1. Written Communication
    2. Verbal Communication
    3. Non-Verbal Communication
- **Three Elements of Effective Verbal Communication**
    1. Listening
    2. Talking
    3. Self-control
- **The Foundation of Communication**
    1. Communication that God commends
    2. Communication that God condemns

The Definition of Communication

Communication is the giving and receiving of information.

That seems simple enough, but I want to point out the different types of communication.

Three Main Types of Communication

1. Written Communication

Throughout history people have gone to great lengths to communicate with one another in writing. Written communication is very important. In fact, the Bible is God's written communication us. Look at **John 20:30-31.** And many other signs truly did Jesus in the presence of his disciples, which are not written in this book: 31 But *these are written, that ye might believe that Jesus is the Christ, the Son of God; and that believing ye might have life through his name*.

John clearly communicates to us in his writing the main reason he wrote his book.

2. Verbal Communication

Verbal communication is the very first form of communication that we read about in the Bible (Genesis 1:28-30). Verbal communication is the most important type of communication within the marriage relationship. It is verbal communication that enables a husband to "dwell with" his wife "according to knowledge." (**1 Peter 3:7**)

3. Non-Verbal Communication

Non-verbal communication is communication that is expressed in body language. The expressions on a persons face, gestures, the way a person carries himself, etc. is "body language." We need only to look at **Genesis 4:5-6** to see that God noted Cain's anger by the look of his countenance (face).

In summary, communication includes written, verbal and non-verbal communication.

Three Elements of Effective Verbal Communication

Communication does not take place unless the following three components are present – **listening, talking, and self-control.** These three components are pointed out in **James 1:19** – *Wherefore, my beloved brethren, let every man be swift to hear, slow to speak, slow to wrath:*

Little or no communication takes place unless someone listens and someone speaks! If you talk and no one is listening, there is no communication. If you listen and no one is willing to talk there is no communication. But that's not all. There can be talking and listening but when anger enters the picture, effective communication ceases! Effective communication only takes place when there is **listening and talking** in the context of **self-control**. (See **Acts 7:51-60**).

In summary, there are three elements in effective communication – listening, talking, and self-control.

The Foundation of Communication

Communication that God commends is based on **truth**. When we communicate with others our discussion must be truthful. This is clearly indicated in **Ephesians 4:25** *Wherefore putting away lying, speak every man truth with his neighbour: for we are members one of another.* **Titus 2:8** refers to truthful communication in these words – *Sound speech, that cannot be condemned..."*

✓Communication that God condemns

Colossians 3:8 *But now ye also put off all these; anger, wrath, malice, blasphemy, <u>filthy communication out of your mouth</u>.*

The language that comes spewing out of the mouths of those who profess to be believers when they are angry distresses me! Filthy, vile communication is not acceptable communication. It MUST be put off! It has no place in the life of a believer! (See **Luke 6:45**)

Ephesians 4:29 *Let no <u>corrupt communication</u> proceed out of your mouth, but that which is good to the use of edifying, that it may minister grace unto the hearers.*

Corrupt communication is a reference to that which is tainted. So what would fit into the category of corrupt communication?

✓Communication tainted by deceit

Deceit is concealing or perverting the truth for the purpose of misleading someone. **1 Peter 3:10** warns us against deceitfulness in our communication. The verse says, *For he that will love life, and see good days, let him refrain his tongue from evil, and his lips that they speak no guile:* The word *guile* is a translation of the Greek word dolos (dol'-os; 1388) meaning to trick or bait with the intention to deceive.

✓Communication tainted by exaggeration

Exaggeration is to magnify or enlarge something beyond the bounds of truth. It is to overstate the facts. People often resort to exaggeration in an effort to get their own way.

Let's call exaggeration what it is...lying. **Colossians 3:9** *Lie not one to another, seeing that ye have put off the old man with his deeds;*

In summary, God commends or approves of truthful communication. He condemns or disproves of filthy communication (swearing, taking His name in vain, filthy talking) and corrupt communication (deceit and exaggeration).

When it comes to communication, our prayer should be – **Psalms 19:14** *Let the words of my mouth, and the meditation of my heart, be acceptable in thy sight, O LORD, my strength, and my redeemer.*

Three Keys for Good Listening

As we have seen, there is no communication if there is no listening. But I want to go one step further. Good communication requires good listening. Below are three keys for good listening…

- **Let The Other Person Speak Without Interruption**

Proverbs 18:13 *He that answereth a matter before he heareth it, it is folly and shame unto him.*

- **Pay Close Attention To What Is Being Said**

James 1:19 *Wherefore, my beloved brethren, let every man be swift to hear, slow to speak, slow to wrath:*

Good listening involves giving the person you are seeking to communicate with your undivided attention. If possible, stop what you are doing and concentrate on what the other person is saying. On occasion I will even jot down notes as the other person is speaking so I am able to more accurately remember what is being said.

- **Be Sure You Understand What The Other Person Is Saying**

1 Peter 3:7 *Likewise, ye husbands, dwell with them according to knowledge...*

I have found it is a good idea to ask some clarifying questions, to be sure that you understand what is being said. Because sometimes what the other person says is not the same as what you understand them to have said. This is illustrated by Christ's conversation with the Jews in **John 2:19-21** *Jesus answered and said unto them, Destroy this temple, and in three days I will raise it up. 20 Then said the Jews, Forty and six years was this temple in building, and wilt thou rear it up in three days? 21 But he spake of the temple of his body.* Yet another illustration of misunderstanding what Christ said is found in **Mark 8:14-16** *Now the disciples had forgotten to take bread, neither had they in the ship with them more than one loaf. 15 And he charged them, saying, Take heed, beware of the leaven of the Pharisees, and of the leaven of Herod. 16 And they reasoned among themselves, saying, It is because we have no bread.*

My point is simply this. Be sure you understand what is being said to you. Sometimes I will repeat back, in summary form, what I understand the other person is saying to me. If they agree with your summary, you can be reasonably sure you are on the same "wave length."

In summary, a good listener...

1) Listens without interrupting

2) Gives the person who is speaking his/her undivided attention

3) Checks to be sure he/she understands what is being communicated

Four Keys For Good Speaking

- **Think Before You Speak**

Proverbs 15:28 *The heart of the righteous studieth to answer: but the mouth of the wicked poureth out evil things.*
Proverbs 29:11 & 20 *A fool uttereth all his mind: but a wise man keepeth it in till afterwards. 20 Seest thou a man that is hasty in his words? there is more hope of a fool than of him.*

When you want to talk to your spouse, especially when you want to work on some important issue, take the time to think about what you want to say. Formulate your point clearly. Be specific not general, and then try to stick with the issue and don't get sidetracked.

- **Choose The Proper Time To Speak**

Ecclesiastes 3:1 & 7 *To every thing there is a season, and a time to every purpose under the heaven: 7 A time to rend, and a time to sew; a time to keep silence, and a time to speak;*
Proverbs 15:23 *A man hath joy by the answer of his mouth: and a word spoken in due season, how good is it!*

- **Exhibit The Right Attitude When You Are Speaking**

How you say something is just as important as what you say. We are instructed to speak the truth in love, and to be kind (Eph. 4:15; 32). When we are dealing with a situation where someone has erred, meekness is to be exhibited (Gal. 6:1). That is not to say that we do not deal with the problems that arise or stand for the truth in the midst of compromise. **Colossians 4:6** articulates the proper attitude that we are to have when we talk with others about important matters – *Let your speech be alway with grace, seasoned with salt, that ye may know how ye ought to answer every man.*

- **Be Constructive Not Destructive In What You Say**

Ephesians 4:29 *Let no corrupt communication proceed out of your mouth, but that which is good to the use of edifying, that it may minister grace unto the hearers.*
God never intended that we engage in destructive criticism and yet allows, and even encourages constructive criticism. There is a vast difference. Two verses come to mind in this area. Both of them are found in Proverbs 27 –

Proverbs 27:6 & 17 *Faithful are the wounds of a friend; but the kisses of an enemy are deceitful. 17 Iron sharpeneth iron; so a man sharpeneth the countenance of his friend.*

Those who engage in constructive criticism want to make the other better. Problem is, many married couples engage in destructive criticism. This is not right. In fact, it is sin.

In summary, a good communicator…

1) Thinks before he/she speaks
2) Chooses the proper time to speak
3) Exhibits the right attitude when he/she speaks
4) Is constructive and not destructive in what he/she says

Pitfalls A Good Communicator Avoids

Indifference – Communication is a **must** in marriage! You cannot afford to be preoccupied or have an "I don't care" attitude.

Temper flare-ups – Proverbs 14:17, 29
Quarreling – Proverbs 17:14; 20:3; 1 Peter 3:9
Abusive, cutting words – Job 19:2; Proverbs 12:18
Harsh words – Proverbs 15:1; 25:15
Mocking – Proverbs 22:10
Offensive Comparisons – Proverbs 18:19
Nagging – Proverbs 21:9; 27:15
Boasting & "Know it all" attitude – Proverbs 27:2; 14:3
Having to get in the last word – Proverbs 26:20-21

God's Blueprint For Good Communication – Listen And Talk With Self Control! How Well Are You Communicating?

Don't bother me with the FACTS! MY MIND IS MADE UP!!!

CHAPTER 5

GOD'S BLUEPRINT FOR COMMITMENT

Psalms 127:1 *Except the LORD build the house, they labour in vain that build it: except the LORD keep the city, the watchman waketh but in vain.*

Hillary Clinton tells us, "It takes a village to raise a child." She goes on to stress that the Government needs to assume a broader roll in rearing children in our culture. That just is not right. Allow me to offer this quote –

> "Governments can't raise children – people do, and the people that bring children into this world should all bear responsibility for raising them."

Do you know who made that statement? President Bill Clinton. Though I seldom agree on family matters with President Clinton, I do agree with him on this quote, because it lines up with the Bible's teaching on child rearing. The parents, both parents, are responsible for rearing that child. **What it takes to raise a child is a dad and a mom working together under the direction of the Lord!**

Our nation is in trouble! One primary reason is because Americans have moved away from the biblical model of the family. Increasingly mothers are off working and dads are absent or playing hooky. Just where does that leave the kids? Who is training the kids? We should not have to be reminded that the family is the foundational building block of society.

The family was the first institution established by God (**Genesis 2:18-25; 1:27-28**). For years no credible person would deny that. Politicians, whether republican or democrat, affirmed the importance of the family. And, they defined the family biblically (i.e. a male father, female mother united in the bond of marriage, procreating and rearing children). Let me offer an example. A number of years back Hubert Humphrey said in his address to the Smithsonian Institution –

"You begin with the family, which is the basic social institution of all civilization, and of all humanity...the family unit is as vital today as it was 200, 500, 1000, yea, 10,000 years ago. And I don't care how many TV sets or how many fast cars you have, or how many theaters, or how many museums, or how many cultural institutions you have... unless you have the will to make the family unit an operating institution of love and understanding, of education and communication, of fellowship and sharing, then all of this is for naught... Those of us who recognize this importance accept the responsibility for taking the steps that are necessary to preserve the family's moral foundation. And, we have no time to spare.

Let me ask you a question. **Are you willing to accept the responsibility for taking the steps that are necessary to preserve the family's moral foundation?**

STEPS NECESSARY TO PRESERVE THE FAMILY

The husband is the head of the wife and charged to rule his own house well (**Eph. 5:23; 1 Tim 3:4**), I am going to emphasize the role of the husband/father. But, the wife/mother has the same responsibility as well. My focus is going to be on commitment. **You cannot have a strong family without commitment**. Commitment is necessary to preserve the family.

COMMITMENT DEFINED

Commit comes from the Latin word which means *to bind together*. When I think of commitment I think of a rope and **Ecclesiastes 4:12** which says in part, *"a threefold cord is not quickly broken."*

I want to use the *threefold cord* to illustrate three essential commitments within the family.

- **Commitment To Christ And The Will of God**
Since it is God who instituted the family, it is only reasonable that He has a central part in family life. Commitment to God begins with Salvation. Three Bible passages need to be pointed out here –
Ephesians 2:8-9; Romans 10:9-13; Ephesians 1:12-13

When we commit ourselves to Christ, Christ commits himself to us. **2 Timothy 1:12** *For the which cause I also suffer these things: nevertheless I am not ashamed: for I know whom I have believed, and am persuaded that he is able to keep that which I have committed unto him against that day.*

Not only do we need to commit our souls to Christ in Salvation, but we also need to commit ourselves to doing the will of God. **Psalms 143:10** *Teach me to do thy will; for thou art my God: thy spirit is good; lead me into the land of uprightness.*

A husband and a father who is committed to the Lord Jesus Christ and to doing the will of God is walking in the light. (**1 John 1:7**). This brings great stability into marriage and family life. There is not the instability and fighting that results in double-mindedness, when the dad (or mom) vacillates between doing their own thing and doing the will of God (**James 1:8; James 4:1-8**).

- **Commitment To Your Wife**
  Proverbs 18:22 *Whoso findeth a wife findeth a good thing, and obtaineth favour of the LORD.*

God created a wife to be a companion, completer, helper and friend. And once you have chosen the woman for your wife, marriage brings you into a life time commitment to her. Therefore, the second strand in the threefold cord of commitment is permanent commitment to your wife.

Have you ever really studied **Matthew 19:3-10**? Most of us are familiar with **Matthew 19:6b** *What therefore God hath joined together, let not man put asunder.* But Christ hits the "marital commitment" issue head on and tells it like it is. Let's look at this passage (read the passage). We are talking permanent commitment here.

I want to emphasize the disciples' conclusion in verse 10 – *"His disciples say unto him, If the case of the man be so with his wife, it is not good to marry."* The point is, marriage is a lifetime commitment (**Romans 7:2-3**)! Now, when I speak of commitment I am not referring to some form of passive past commitment that was based on hormones and emotions. Rather, I am referring to the daily exercise of **1 Corinthians 13** love. I am referring to taking the time to get to know your wife and communicate with her (**1 Peter 3:7-10**). I am talking about building the kind of a relationship together so that you enjoy being together and that after years of marriage you are still ravished with her love (**Proverbs 5:18-21**).

This kind of relationship requires personal effort and investing time.

- **Commitment To Your Children**

The final strand in the threefold cord is a commitment to your children. Look at **Ephesians 6:4.** Notice what the father is charged with in the context of child rearing. That is no accident! Fathers are to be active in the rearing of their children. **Ephesians 6:4** *And, ye fathers, provoke not your children to wrath: but bring them up in the nurture and admonition of the Lord.*

One of the things that your wife needs the most, if there are children still at home, is your consistent involvement in the instruction and discipline of those children. The Book of Proverbs is filled with a father's instruction to his children. I was at my son's home just last night for a "father's day meal." When we were done I helped him replace a water pump on his car. As we were working together, he looked at me and said, "thanks dad, for teaching me how to use tools and do things like this. You have saved me literally hundreds of dollars." I can tell you, those words were a blessing to me!

Men and women, our nation and our churches desperately need strong families. One key aspect of developing a strong family is **COMMITMENT** –

1) Commitment to the Lord & His Will
2) Commitment to Your Wife
3) Commitment to Your Children

Examine Your Commitments!

CHAPTER 6
GOD'S BLUEPRINT FOR PARENTS

Review

God has a blueprint, as it were, for marriage and family relationships. This "blueprint," revealing God's will for the family, is clearly revealed in the Bible. God has a will for husbands, wives, parents and children. So far, we have considered...

- **God's Will For The Husband**
    It is God's will that every husband <u>love his wife</u> (Eph. 5:25, 28, 33) and <u>lead his wife</u> (Eph. 5:23; 1 Cor. 11:3; Gen. 3:16).

- **God's Will For The Wife**
    It is God's will that every wife <u>submits to her husband</u> (Eph. 5:22-23 & 33) and it is God's will that the wife <u>help, assist and complete her husband</u> (Gen. 2:18-22).

Next, we move on to...

- **God's Will For Parents**
    It is God's will for all parents that they <u>rear their children Biblically</u> (Prov. 22:6; Eph. 6:4)

Three of the most delightful experiences of our lives have been when Linda gave birth to Steven, Karla and Sarah. I was present and assisted (in a minor way) in their birthing. I can't recall any other events that have been more anxious but exhilarating, frightening yet exciting, agonizing yet joyful, exhausting (for Linda) yet pleasurable than the birth of our 3 children. We indeed count *"the fruit of the womb"* as *"his reward."*

But, we soon realized that, contrary to what some people think, (usually people who have not had children), that children are not "little angels."

The Biblical View of A Child's Nature

Psalms 51:5 *Behold, I was shapen in iniquity, and in sin did my mother conceive me.*

Psalms 58:3 *The wicked are estranged from the womb: they go astray as soon as they be born, speaking lies.* **Note**: From the moment of birth, children are *estranged* from God and his righteousness. Simply stated, they are sinners!

Ephesians 2:3 *Among whom also we all had our conversation in times past in the lusts of our flesh, fulfilling the desires of the flesh and of the mind; and were by nature the children of wrath, even as others.* **Note**: The phrase *by nature* literally means by birth. Children, by birth are sinners, destined to be subject to the wrath of God. The unsaved person is condemned already (**John 3:18**). The sentence has been passed, yet God, in His mercy is staying the execution of the sentence to give people the opportunity to personally trust Christ (**2 Peter 3:8-9**). In fact, what I am saying is that children do not naturally do what is right! They do not naturally make the right choices in life. They do not anxiously follow that which is right, holy and good. In fact, **Proverbs 22:15a** tells us, *Foolishness is bound in the heart of a child..."* not righteousness. Since this is true, what are parents to do?

There are some who suggest that "they are just going through a stage which they will eventually grow out of." That is just not true! The Bible says, *The rod and reproof give wisdom: but a child left to himself bringeth his mother to shame.* **Proverbs 29:15**

That brings me to the parents. God makes it clear in his Word that he expects parents to bring up children, and not let them go their own way.

God's Will For Parents

- **It is God's will that parents rear their children biblically**

Proverbs 22:6 *Train up a child in the way he should go: and when he is old, he will not depart from it.*
The command given here is to parents. Parents are to train their children in the way they **should go,** not the way **they want to go.**
But, the question is, what *way* should they go? We find that answer in **Ephesians 6:4** *And, ye fathers, provoke not your children to wrath: but bring them up in the nurture and admonition of the Lord.* The word **nurture** is the translation of a Greek word which refers to the teaching of children which includes the disciplinary correction of them. The word **admonition** comes from the Greek word which means to call attention to by warning, admonishing and counseling. So, here's what we have. Fathers are told that it is their responsibility to instruct, disciple, warn and counsel their children according to the principles the LORD has given to us. And we know that those principles are revealed in the Bible...

1) Teach them the 2 Commandments of the Lord (Mat. 2:37-40)
2) Teach them the Scriptures and their need of a Savior (2 Tim. 3:15)
3) Teach them to obey you (Eph. 6:1)
4) Teach them to flee youthful lusts and follow righteousness, etc. (2 Tim. 2:22)
5) Teach them to walk in the Spirit (Gal. 5:16 & ff)

One more question I want to answer. How long are parents to do this? This is revealed in the phrase **bring them up**. That is one word in the Greek – εκτρεφετε – *ektrepho* (ek-tref'-o; 1625). The word means to train up to maturity. Simply stated, God holds parents responsible for the instruction, disciplining, warning and counseling their children until they come to maturity, which was generally considered to be when they were of marriageable age.

As a matter of clarification, I want to make it clear that both parents are to be involved in bringing up the children. The Scriptures make that clear. Note these two examples –

Proverbs 1:8 *My son, hear the instruction of thy father, and forsake not the law of thy mother:*

Proverbs 6:20 *My son, keep thy father's commandment, and forsake not the law of thy mother:*

To be sure dad is to be the head of the house (1 Timothy 3:5) but mom is to be the primary *keeper* at home (Titus 2:5). [Note: the phrase *"keepers at home..."* is a translation of the Greek word οικουρους, *oikouros* (oy-koo-ros'; 3626) which means a stayer at home; one who guards or looks after the affairs of the home.

God's Will For Parents Is To Rear Their Children Biblically!

But what if you have an unsaved spouse? Paul gives us insight into this situation in **1 Corinthians 7:12-14** *But to the rest speak I, not the Lord: If any brother hath a wife that believeth not, and she be pleased to dwell with him, let him not put her away. 13 And the woman which hath an husband that believeth not, and if he be pleased to dwell with her, let her not leave him. 14 For the unbelieving husband is sanctified by the wife, and the unbelieving wife is sanctified by the husband: else were your children unclean; but now are they holy.* This passage clearly states that the believing spouse can have a sanctifying influence on the children, even if the other spouse is an unbeliever. A wonderful example of this is pointed out by Paul in **2 Timothy 1:5** *When I call to remembrance the unfeigned faith that is in thee, which dwelt first in thy grandmother Lois, and thy mother Eunice; and I am persuaded that in thee also.* Evidently Timothy's father was unsaved. But grandma and mom pointed Timothy to Christ. While there is no doubt that this is difficult, particularly when the wife is married to an unsaved husband, Eunice is an example of the influence a Christian mother can have.

If both the husband and wife are believers, it is extremely important that you are together in the rearing of your children. You need to be supportive of each other. You must not undermine each other in the training and discipline of your children. In order for that to happen you must communicate regularly with each other about your children.

Three Tips That Will Help You Rear Your Children Biblically

There are three thoughts that I will share with you that can help you rear your children biblically...

1. **Realize That You Are Your Child's Hero, Dad**
2. **Communicate With Your Children Constantly**
3. **Love Your Children Fervently**

Let's look at each of these individually.

- **Dads, Realize That You Are Your Child's First Hero, Therefore Live A Consistent Christian Life Before Them**

Proverbs 17:6 *Children's children are the crown of old men; and the glory* (boast) *of children are their fathers.*

This verse tells us that dads are the heroes of their young children! That certainly was true of me. I loved to brag about my dad when I was a kid. He was "the greatest" in my eyes. I can even remember pretending I was my dad. I'd put on his fireman's helmet, jump in the fire truck (my bicycle) and race off to fight the fire and save the people, just like my dad. Dad was my hero. I talked about him and his exploits often to the other kids. We have had some great times together and I have learned a lot from my dad.

Dads, your young children look at you as their hero and protector. That is a weighty responsibility. In light of that responsibility, you need to be the right kind of hero or role model. And, you need to take advantage of your position and model Christian character and conduct before your children. Young boys and girls, for the most part, determine what a "real man" is, based upon the example of their fathers. For this reason, make sure that your children see in you...Real men make Christ first priority in their lives; Real men read their Bibles; Real men pray; Real men go to church; Real men are active public witnesses for Christ; Real men love their wives; Real men take time for their children, etc.

A wise father takes his position as "hero" or primary role model seriously and seeks to live a consistent Christian life before his children.

- **Communicate With Your Children Constantly, Teaching Them To Love The Lord And Live For Him**

Read **Deuteronomy 6:3-15**.

Noah Webster (1758-1843), whom American history refers to as *"the Schoolmaster of the Nation,"* was on the right track when he said, *"Education is useless without the Bible...God's Word, contained in the Bible, has furnished all the necessary rules to direct our conduct."*

Parents, one of the most important tasks you have, when it comes to rearing your children, is to open a line of communication with your children early so that you can begin etching upon your child's mind the words and principles of the Bible. This is important for at least two reasons. 1) It is the Scriptures that will point your child to Christ and Heaven (**2 Tim. 3:15**) instead of Satan and Hell. 2) It is the Scriptures that will program your child's moral compass (**Psa. 119:9-11**).

When should you begin? Begin as soon as the child is born! Talk to them and be sure to talk to them about the Lord. Sing to them and include biblical songs. Read Bible stories to them and the Bible itself. Pray with them. When they get old enough to begin talking to you, be sure to listen to them and respond to them. Moms, when they go to school, one of the best and most important times to talk with your children is as soon as they walk in the door. You can learn a lot about your child and what's going on in his/her life if you talk to them as soon as they come home from school.

There are other good times to talk to your kids as well. Two major times in our home where communication took place was around the supper table and at bedtime. Keep in mind that you need to use the Bible as the yardstick for measuring behavior and setting family guidelines. Around our supper table we would talk about some of the following things…

1. Share our testimonies of how we came to Christ
2. Talk about what Salvation is and why we need to be saved
3. Note Godly or ungodly character in our discussions
4. Share how to handle life situations biblically
5. Pose hypothetical situations and then explain how to respond biblically
6. Discuss the meaning of Bible words and passages and then tell how we can put them into practice in our own lives
7. Pray together
8. Read the Bible together

Just a quick note about bedtime…I talked to, and told stories to my children well into their teenage years. I had fun with them by telling them little stories. Sometimes they were silly, and often I used them as a teaching tool. They looked forward to this time and I miss it, yet to this day. God used this time to knit our family together. After the story, we would pray and tuck them in.

Parents, if you are going to rear your children biblically you need to take every opportunity to communicate with your children, teaching them to love the Lord Jesus Christ and to live for Him. Your most important mission is to point your child to Salvation in Christ and then to teach them how to live for the Lord.

- **Love Your Children Fervently**

Children need to know that their parents love them. This needs to be seen in the parent's actions and spoken by their words. Paul told Titus that the older women were to teach the younger woman to love their children (**Titus 2:4**). We know that dads are to love their children as well, because we are instructed to *"turn away"* from men who are *"without natural affection"* (**2 Tim. 3:3 &5**). The phrase *"without natural affection"* is a translation of the Greek word αστοργοι - *astorgos* (as'-tor-gos; 794) which means **one who does not love his family**. Dads, your children need the security of hearing that they are loved! Wise fathers tell their children often, "I love you!"

To be sure, loving your children is more than just the expression of words. Acts of kindness and involvement, a hug and kiss, proper loving touches, etc. are all important expressions of love. Loving your children also includes setting clear boundaries for expected behavior (**Prov. 22:6**). Children should be praised when they obey, and disciplined (including spanking) when the child breaches that boundary (**Prov. 13:24**). It is unloving to allow your children to be rowdy, rebellious and undisciplined. Our society is reaping a crop to violence today, because parents have refused to discipline their children biblically. Love your children enough to establish clear, consistent, understandable boundaries in attitude and conduct and then spank them soundly when they cross the line.

Summary

I have shared three thoughts that will help you bring up your children biblically, according to **Ephesians 6:4** *And, ye fathers, provoke not your children to wrath: but bring them up in the nurture and admonition of the Lord.*

- Realize That You Are Your Child's Hero, Dad, Therefore Live A Consistent Christian Life Before Them
- Communicate With Your Children Constantly, Teaching Them To Love The Lord And Live For Him
- Love Your Children Fervently, Expressing It In Actions And Words

> **God's Will For Parents Is To Rear Their Children Biblically. To Accomplish This, You need Christ! Is He Your Savior?**

CHAPTER 7

GOD'S BLUEPRINT FOR CHILDREN

Youth gangs are an increasing problem in our culture. Last summer an Oak Creek family put up a new wooden fence and within 48 hours of its completion, it had gang symbols painted all over it. Youth gangs are responsible for thefts, rapes, assault, drug sales, murder and more. I know for a fact that there are kids in my church who have been pressured to become a part of a gang. One of the members of this church has produced a video on the gang problem. We have used that video in our Time Out Ministry.

One of the hallmark characteristics of gangs is that they have no respect for parents or authority figures. They despise anyone in the place of authority and become an authority unto themselves and even spurn the authority of God! I must warn you parents, this attitude begins early in children and if not corrected you will have big trouble on your hands even before your child is a teenager.

I want to share with you a shocking true story about a youth gang and how that God judged that gang because of their lack of respect for a man of God. There were 42 gang members in this gang and they were all in their early teens, most likely. A preacher was out for a walk. As he passed by the woods, these kids poured out and surrounded him.

Have you ever been in a situation like that? I can tell you from experience, it is frightening. A situation something like that happened to Linda, Steve, Karla and I one time. We had just come out of church and I hailed a driver to take us home. As we were walking to where he was parked, a young mother came out with a sickly looking baby. She was asking me for money to help her baby. I reached into my pocket and pulled out a small bill and handed it to her. That is when things got out of hand. Before we knew it, people poured out from the allies and from behind houses and we were literally surrounded. They were all pushing us until they had us backed up against the car. I was fearful for my wife and our two young kids. The driver managed to get the door open. I shoved my wife and Karla in and threw Steve in. I managed to get in and wrench the door from grasping hands as the driver pulled away. He scolded me and warned me never to do that again. I can tell you, that is high on my list of life's most frightening experiences.

Now back to the original story, these 42 gang members surrounded this preacher. They began to mock him and ridicule him. They even knocked him down and then taunted him saying, get up baldy, get up! Then they backed off. Well, that preacher did get up, turned to face the rowdy gang, headed right toward them and stared right at them. Then he did something that shocked them. He told them that their conduct was reprehensible before God and that God would judge them because of it. Before the gang could respond, two she bears came out of the woods and attacked the gang members. All 42 of them were torn to shreds.

This is a true story my friends. God does not take lightly those who mock their parents, preachers, or those in rightful authority. Before we move on, I want to document the account I have just shared with you. Read **2 Kings 2:23-24**.

- **God's Will For Children Is That They Honor Their Parents!**

That brings me to my first point. It is **God's will that a child honor his parents.** Now, you might be wondering, what does this have to do with the above illustration about the youth gangs? Let me make it clear if children do not honor their parents, it is unlikely that they will honor any other authority, not even God!

Young people, listen to me. It is God's will that you honor your parents. The fifth of the Ten Commandments says, *Honour thy father and thy mother: that thy days may be long upon the land which the LORD thy God giveth thee.* **Exodus 20:12.** Eight times this commandment is repeated in the Bible.

What Does "Honor" Mean?

In the Noah Webster's 1828 dictionary, *honor* is defined – To revere; to respect; to treat with deference and submission. This lines up with the Hebrew and Greek word translated honor. It is God's will that children honor their parents. Look at **Leviticus 19:3** *Ye shall fear every man his mother, and his father, and keep my sabbaths: I am the LORD your God.*

The word *fear* in this verse is the Hebrew word yare' (yaw-ray; 3372) which implies such high respect for someone that you would have great apprehension about doing something that would displease them. Read Leviticus 19:3 again. You can tell if a young person honors their parents, because, if they do they will not regularly do anything that would displease them. This attitude pleases God! God honors children that honor their parents.

BUT, what about those who dishonor their parents? The Bible has plenty to say about that...

Deuteronomy 27:16 *Cursed be he that setteth light by his father or his mother. And all the people shall say, Amen.*

The phrase *"setteth light"* means to esteem lightly or to pay little or no attention to. The word *"cursed"* means to execrate. Now that is not a word we use today. "Execrate" means to pronounce a curse or pronounce evil against. God says that those who do not honor their parents are cursed. They are headed for evil, because he will put evil in their path.

Now, just in case you are inclined to ignore this passage because it is Old Testament, consider **Matthew 15:4** *For God commanded, saying, Honour thy father and mother: and, He that curseth* (revile or speak evil of or to) *father or mother, let him die the death.* Let me make it clear what this passage means. Any young person who refused to respect and obey his parents was worthy of the death penalty (see Ex. 21:17 & Lev. 20:9).

I will say it again. God's will for children is that they honor their parents. **Ephesians 6:2** says, *Honour thy father and mother; which is the first commandment with promise;*

Helping Parents In Their Old Age
There is another way which grown children are to honor their parents in their old age, that is to help them and if necessary care for them. There are numerous verses that point out this responsibility.

Matthew 15:5-6 *But ye say, Whosoever shall say to his father or his mother, It is a gift, by whatsoever thou mightest be profited* (helped) *by me; 6 And honour not his father or his mother, he shall be free. Thus have ye made the commandment of God of none effect by your tradition.*

1 Timothy 5:4 *But if any widow* have *children or nephews, let them learn first to show piety* (to care for) *at home, and to requite* (repay) *their parents: for that is good and acceptable before God.*

Proverbs 23:22 *Hearken unto thy father that begat thee, and despise not thy mother when she is old.*

There is one last verse that I want to share with you – **Leviticus 19:32** *Thou shalt rise up before the hoary* (gray or white) *head, and honour the face of the old man, and fear thy God: I am the LORD.*

- **It Is God's Will That Children Obey Their Parents**

Ephesians 6:1 *Children, obey your parents in the Lord: for this is right. 2 Honour thy father and mother; which is the first commandment with promise;*

Colossians 3:20 *Children, obey your parents in all things: for this is well pleasing unto the Lord.*

See also Proverbs 1:8-16; Proverbs 6:20-23

It is God's will that children obey their parents. Now, I must say that there is one exception to this rule. If a parent asked you to sin against what the Bible says, then you must obey God (Acts 5:29).

**God's Will For All Children Is to Honor
And Obey Their Parents.**

CHAPTER 8

KEEP THE HOME FIRES BURNING!

Counsel for Maintaining a Strong, Vibrant Marriage

7 Suggestions for Maintaining a Strong, Vibrant Marriage

1. **Companionship**
2. **Commitment**
3. **Communication**
4. **Expressing Appreciation**
5. **Responsibility & Forgiveness**
6. **Romance**
7. **Active Spiritual Involvement**

There are some wonderful things you just don't forget about your childhood. One of those pleasant memories was hurrying down to the kitchen on cold winter mornings and feeling the warm floor under my cold feet. The century old home that we lived in was well kept and roomy but not very well insulated. I had an upstairs bedroom and in the winter it got plenty cool by the time morning came. The worst part was getting out from under the pile of blankets and putting my bare feet on the cold floor. I did not waste any time getting to the kitchen because we knew the Round Oak wood stove in the basement would be fired up and the floors would be warm.

I sure enjoyed the warmth. It was wonderful. But it did not come about without effort. My dad cut and split wood regularly throughout the year. It was my job to carry the wood to the basement. Dad would start the fire before he went to work and mom would put wood on the fire to keep it going. As I think back, it took a lot of effort to keep that fire going, but it was worth it considering the alternative...cold feet! We **all** enjoyed the warmth and so we **all** did our part to keep the home fires burning.

Keeping the fire going in the wood stove is much like keeping the love alive in your marriage; it does not "just happen." You have to work at it. You must add fuel to the "love fires" to keep them burning. Unfortunately, married folks are forgetting that and it is evident. One survey says "6 of every 12 marriages become loveless, utilitarian relationships sustained to protect children, property, shared careers and other business interests." In other words, COLD!

A cold, utilitarian relationship does not appeal to me! A WARM, LOVING RELATIONSHIP ranks high on my list of priorities. How about you? If you want to kindle the coals of love in your marriage relationship, the following recommendations will add fuel to the fire. It will take effort, but when you consider the alternative it is worth it!

1. COMPANIONSHIP

Marriage counselor Norman Wright notes that, *"...within each of us is the hunger for contact, acceptance, belonging, intimate exchange, responsiveness, support, love and the touch of tenderness."* A caring spouse can help fill that need so we do not have to feel lonely. God planned it that way when he created Adam. **Genesis 2:18** says, "It is not good that the man should be alone; I will make him an help meet for him."

Simply stated, God made Adam a companion suited for him. Neither a beautiful environment nor a variety of animals would fill the bill. A man's best friend is NOT to be his dog! It should be his wife.

Marriage, right from the start, was to be a relationship based on mutual, compassionate companionship. Marriage was NEVER designed to be a dictator-doormat relationship. Paul makes this clear when he begins talking about husband and wife relationships by saying "submitting yourselves one to another..." in **Ephesians 5:21**. What does that mean? The husband submits by being the loving leader of his wife and the wife submits by obeying her husband and putting her energies into him to make him successful.

Couples who want to keep the home fires burning will make time for each other and that time will be quality time. Be sure to talk together, work together on projects of mutual interest, play together, and dream together.

When I was dating my wife to be, we saw each other every chance we could. We worked opposite shifts which made things difficult but NOT impossible. **The key was we made time for each other**.

Too often, once the knot has been tied, the wife is left isolated. The husband is off at work or with the boys while the wife is working, keeping up with the kids, and minding "the castle." Though in this 21st century I see more of the wife being off with the girls and cold toward her husband as well.

Wise couples will carve out time to be with each other. They will **make nurturing their relationship a prime priority** despite the job obligations, children, community and church commitments. WHY? Caring for each other and being with each other is the fuel that keeps the relationship warm.

There is a second suggestion I want to share with you that will keep your marriage warm...

2. COMMITMENT

Commitment is the cornerstone of strong marriages. God's blueprint for marriage is clearly drawn in the Bible. It is, **One Man plus One Woman for One Lifetime. Matthew 19:6** points out the importance of complete commitment when it says, "What God has joined together, let not man put asunder."

Far too many couples come to the marriage altar with selfish, unrealistic expectations. Each person is focusing on **what they can GET** out of marriage instead of considering what they MUST give to make the marriage work. A successful marriage is an exercise in GIVING.

Know this: **There are no "story book" marriages**. If you hear of a marriage that is "perpetual bliss" it is a fairy tale. Why? Because **there are no perfect husbands and no perfect wives**. All marriages have their strengths and weaknesses, their good times and their difficult times, their highs and their lows.

So **what keeps a marriage going**? The secret fuel that keeps the love fires burning is the total commitment of each marriage partner to the other. By total commitment I mean, **the willingness to hang in there and work things out, in spite of weaknesses, disappointments and failures**.

I read this definition of a "perfect marriage" – "A Perfect Marriage is just two imperfect people who refuse to give up on each other!"

One author explained commitment like this... "A successful marriage is not one in which two people, beautifully matched find each other and get along happily ever after because of the initial matching. It is, instead, a system by means of which persons who are sinful and contentious are so caught by a dream bigger than themselves that they work throughout the years, in spite of repeated disappointment, to make the dream come true." Make it OBVIOUS to your spouse that you are committed to making your marriage work.

There is another aspect of commitment that needs to be considered. Be committed to being satisfied with your partner. Our society has a morbid preoccupation with what I call *The Septic Tank Syndrome*. Movies, TV, Porn, videos, romance novels, etc. promote the philosophy – *The Grass Is Greener On The Other Side Of The Fence!* When was the last time you saw a TV movie where married people were enjoying a fulfilling relationship with each other? It is an unusual show that does not promote the "grass is greener..." philosophy. But that philosophy is a MYTH! Do you know where the grass is greener? When I was a kid, in our yard, I have found that the grass is always greener over the septic tank. The entertainment media has disguised the hurt, the broken lives and the tragedy of marriages shattered by unfaithfulness. They make adultery look attractive but it is devastating American families.

The wisest man who ever lived wrote in **Proverbs 5:15-23** of the importance of being satisfied with your marriage partner. He said, "Drink water out of thine own cistern... rejoice with the wife of thy youth... let her breasts satisfy thee at all times; and be thou ravished always with her love." He goes on to say how foolish it is to look outside of the marriage relationship for satisfaction. I suggest you get out your Bible and carefully read this passage in its entirety.

Commitment means that **your spouse holds a position of honor in your life**. That means there is a bond of sexual exclusiveness between you.

COMMITTMENT is the fuel that keeps the marriage fires burning.

3. COMMUNICATION

(Charitable Communication)

A lady stopped in her pastor's office one day and as soon as she sat down she was in tears. She said "my husband can't say a kind word to me! I don't know what to do." The problem was tearing her and their marriage apart.

Ephesians 4:15 tells us the importance of "speaking the truth in love." That's what I call charitable communication. Words can be used like weapons. Job of old experienced this first hand and tells of the hurt misused words caused him. He said in **Job 19:2**, "How long will you...break me in pieces with words."

There is an old proverb that says – I "The road to the heart is the ear." I believe that is true. That explains why many marriages are growing cold! **I read that on the average out of the 10,080 plus minutes in every week, the average couple spends only 17 minutes in close communication?** That's the chilling fact.

The Apostle Peter told husbands that they are to "dwell with them (their wives) according to knowledge..." in **I Peter 3:7**. By what he meant, <u>a man needs to get to know his wife</u>. That does not happen by accident. It will take time, time spent in quality communication, time talking and listening.

COMMUNICATION POINTERS

- Remember, how you say something is just as important as what you say.
- Don't forget that "body language" communicates as much as your words.
- Be a good listener, give thought to what you say before you say it and be slow to get angry. (**James 1:19-20 & Proverbs 17:27**)
- Be sure to be truthful but use the truth wrapped in love and not like a weapon. (**Ephesians 4:15**)
- Be courteous, your partner deserves an opportunity to speak without harassment or interruption. (**Proverbs 18:13**)
- Do not resort to EXAGGERATION to support your argument. Exaggeration is inflating the facts beyond the limits of truth. Phrases like, "you always...", "You never..." or "You're just like..." are exaggerations and should be avoided. Exaggerated threats are common also. Exaggeration erodes trust, credibility and hinders communication. (**Ephesians 4:25**)
- Resolve arguments the same day they occur if at all possible so they don't turn into bitterness and resentment. (**Ephesians 2:26**)

If you want to keep the home fires burning, you will need to sharpen your communication skills. Kind communication and lots of it adds necessary fuel that keeps the love fires burning in a marriage.

4. APPRECIATION

I came across a card from American Greetings that illustrates my point beautifully. It was set up like a Want Ad in the newspaper, it said, and I quote...

WANTED: MOTHER

Long hours, low pay, little time off.

Must be willing to work overtime on weekends, holidays, and summer vacation.

Energy, imagination, intelligence, endurance, and flexibility required.

Must have ability to lead, instruct and guide, coupled with a warm and loving, affectionate personality.

On-the-job training offered.

Inside the card said, **THANKS for taking the job, Mom!**

The card could well have applied to a wife or a husband. The point is this. **No one wants to be used**. A husband wants to be more than a pay check and a wife more than a domestic servant. Everyone needs to know they are sincerely appreciated. Just knowing that your spouse cares will go a long way in getting you through tough situations. And it's right, too. Men, appreciation is a part of what it means to "cherish" your wife in **Ephesians 5:29**. Ladies, appreciation is a part of what it means to "reverence" your husband in **Ephesians 5:33**.

Refuse to take your spouse for granted. Kind words of appreciation, lending a helping hand and creative, unexpected actions that show you value and esteem your mate will go a long way in keeping your relationship warm.

There is a fifth suggestion that is perhaps the most important suggestion of all when it comes to keeping the marriage relationship warm.

5. RESPONSIBILITY AND FORGIVENESS

All of us bring "excess baggage" into marriage. That includes personality weaknesses, personal problems, clashing opinions, different ideals, etc. When something goes wrong it is our natural inclination to blame the other person and or "pass the buck." That is wrong. We must take responsibility for our own shortcomings and errors. Though it may be difficult to admit that "I am wrong" or that "I am a part of the problem" it is a part of our obligation to our spouse. It is a necessity and not an option. When you are wrong, you need to be mature enough to own up to it. Both husbands and wives need to put away their pride and learn to say, "I'm sorry." A sincere, heartfelt apology will go a long way in keeping a marriage relationship on track.

There is the other side of the coin that must be looked at also. **That is forgiveness**. Forgiveness is also fuel that keeps the home fires burning and the relationship warm. Now, I know some will protest at this point. Their attitude is similar to what one bitter woman said to her counselor... "It will be a cold day in H--- before I ever forgive my husband. He does not deserve to be forgiven!" Few will be as crass as that woman, but *many hold the same malignant attitude*. That is a MARRIAGE DESTROYING ATTITUDE! **Ephesians 3:13** points out the proper attitude. We are not to hold grudges, but be tolerant and ready to forgive. Note the specific words, "Forbearing one another, and forgiving one another, if any man have a quarrel against any: even as Christ forgave you, so also do ye." Before God, none of us deserve the forgiveness of our sins. But when a person receives Christ as Savior, that person is freely and fully given of his or her sins. Because Christ has forgiven us, we are to forgive others.

When you forgive someone, what does that mean? Dr. Jay Adams says (I am paraphrasing) **First**, it means you are promising and choosing not to use it against the person in the future. **Second**, you are promising and choosing not to talk to others about it. **Lastly**, you are promising and choosing not to dwell on it yourself.

Dispense forgiveness in generous amounts. It pays off.

6. ROMANCE

The sixth suggestion I offer you is, **keep romance alive in your relationship**. Some will say, "Oh come on now, you don't ever find romance mentioned in the Bible."

To be sure, the word "romance" does not appear in the Bible, but illustrations of it do. Read the Song of Solomon or the story of Ruth and Boaz as recorded in the Old Testament Book of Ruth. There you will find romance in all of its purity and excitement.

Did you know that the absence of romantic love is on the top of the heap as a source of depression among married women? While I do not endorse many of the psychological teaching of Dr. James Dobson, I believe he is right on in this observation he made –

"A man can be contented with a kind of business partnership in marriage, provided sexual privileges are a part of the arrangement. As long as the wife prepares dinner each evening, is reasonably amiable, and doesn't nag him during football season, he can be satisfied." But that is not the case with the wife! She yearns to be her husband's Special Sweetheart. She would likely trade the new TV, her dishwasher or just about anything for a single expression of genuine tenderness and attention that does not have to be 'paid for' with sex."

A wise husband will take his wife on dates, remember anniversaries and special days. He will write or text her love notes or get her a small gift for no special reason.

A word of wisdom to the wives. Don't neglect your husbands. Husbands appreciate love notes too. He wants you to be "sexy" for him just as much as you want him to be romantic with you. Don't turn up your nose at that! That's the way most men are wired.

If you want to keep the home fires burning men, you will stimulate romance in your relationship. Ladies, if you want to have a warm marital relationship you will not treat your physical obligation to your husband as a "necessary evil."

There is one final suggestion I want to share with you. It focuses on the spiritual aspect of your relationship.

7. ACTIVE SPIRITUAL INVOLVEMENT

The kind of self-giving love needed to sustain a marriage relationship cannot be generated merely by personal desire, but it is available. The logical question is, "What is the source?" The answer is, "It is available from God, through his Son, Jesus

Christ." The Bible says in **I John 4:8**, "God is love." In order to tap into the reservoir of God's love a person must believe on Jesus Christ. The moment you put your faith in Christ, **Romans 5:5** tells us, "...the love of God is shed abroad in our hearts by the Holy Ghost which is given unto us." At that moment God gives you the desire and the power to initiate the self-giving love needed to sustain your marriage.

Simply stated, spiritual involvement begins with personal faith in the risen Savior, Jesus Christ. Have you ever prayed, admitting to God that you are a sinner? Have you ever asked the Lord to forgive your sins? Have you ever told Christ you believe he died for your sins and arose from the dead? Have you ever personally invited Christ to come into your life and be your Savior from the guilt, penalty and power of sin? If not, why not do it right now. Honestly and reverently come to Jesus Christ confessing that you are a sinner. Express your belief in what the Bible says about Christ: That He, God's only begotten Son, died to pay for my sins and arose from the dead, being alive today. Invite Him into my life this very moment and to be my personal Savior. Thank you for hearing and answering my prayer.

Once you have received Christ, the next step is to get involved in a good, solid, Bible preaching church. That is important to your marriage! A study done by a University of Virginia sociologist found that couples who attend church regularly are 42% more likely to still be married for the first time than those couples who don't attend church. In addition, reading the Bible and praying together regularly is important if you are going to keep the home fires burning.

Wouldn't you agree that the warmth of being in love beats the coldness of a utilitarian relationship? If so, get busy and start stoking the fire with the fuel... 1) Companionship, 2) Commitment, 3) Communication, 4) Expressing Appreciation,

5) Responsibility and Forgiveness, 6) Romance, and 7) Active Spiritual Involvement.

My wife Linda and I were married in 1969. We have 3 children and 13 grandchildren. We have a marriage where the "home fires" are still burning, but that did NOT happen by accident. We work to keep it that way! If you need some help in your marriage. Please get in touch with me.

REVIEW

There is no doubt about it! God has a blueprint for building strong, successful Marriages and Families! He has clearly drawn out that blueprint in the Bible. Let's review God's Blueprint one more time.

1. **God's Blueprint For Married Couples**: It is God's design and will that each married couple **leave** their parents, **cleave** to each other and become intimately involved (**one flesh**) with each other.
2. **God's Blueprint For Husbands**: It is God's design and will that each husband **love** his own wife and **lead** her.
3. **God's Blueprint For Wives**: It is God's design and will that each wife **submit** to her own husband and **assist, aid** and **complete** him.
4. **God's Blueprint For Communication**: It is God's design and will that family members **listen** and **talk** with each other often, within the context of **self-control**.
5. **God's Blueprint For Commitment**: It is God's design and will that each family member be **committed to Christ, spouses be committed to each other**, and **parents be committed to their children**.
6. **God's Blueprint For Parents**: It is God's design and will that each parent **rear their children biblically, communicate with them constantly**, and **love them fervently**.
7. **God's Blueprint For Children**: It is God's design and will that **children obey and honor their parents** when they are young and **honor their parents** when they are old.

8. **Keep The Home Fires Burning**: 7 Suggestions for maintain a strong, vibrant marriage.

I am reminded of what we read in **Matthew 7:24-27** *Therefore whosoever heareth these sayings of mine, and doeth them, I will liken him unto a wise man, which built his house upon a rock: 25 And the rain descended, and the floods came, and the winds blew, and beat upon that house; and it fell not: for it was founded upon a rock. 26 And every one that heareth these sayings of mine, and doeth them not, shall be likened unto a foolish man, which built his house upon the sand: 27 And the rain descended, and the floods came, and the winds blew, and beat upon that house; and it fell: and great was the fall of it.*

Marriages that last, and families that are strong, build according to God's Blueprint. Building on any other foundation is like building on the sand.

The Biblical Equation for Marriage
Marriage = 1 Man + 1 Woman for 1 Lifetime

Dr. David L Brown

P.O. BOX 173
Oak Creek, WI 53154

Phone (414) 768-9754
E-mail – PastorDavidLBrown@gmail.com

Where Will You Spend Eternity?

"Well," you ask, **"how would *I* know?"** Thank God, according to the Bible, not only can you *know*, but you can *choose* where you will spend eternity.

Now we all believe — or at least most claim to believe — in the Bible as God's Word. We believe in eternity and know that life is short. The Bible itself asks, "What is your life? It is even a vapor, that appeareth for a little time, and then vanisheth away" (James 4:14).

Many claim to believe in heaven and in hell, yet, unfortunately, show little concern over their eternal destiny. We are far more concerned about this life than the next, yet we know that eternity is endless. The Word of God describes it as being "forever and ever" (Revelation 22:5).

Just think...an eternity to be spent forever, either in the perfect paradise called heaven or in the terrible torments of hell.

Surely we'll agree that it is just good sense to prepare for eternity now, before it is forever too late. God says, "It is appointed unto men once to die, but after this the judgment" (Hebrews 9:27).

"Well," you say, "I believe in God, go to church, and live the best I can. What else can I do?"

Now believing in God, attending church, and doing one's best are all admirable; yet, according to the Word of God, the Holy Bible, these *cannot* get us to heaven. Neither, according to God, can our church membership, baptism, confirmation, nor our good deeds attain for us eternal life.

But God has provided an answer to the matter of life and death, heaven and hell. It is an answer so simple it is frequently overlooked.

A religious leader named Nicodemus came to Jesus one night for help. Jesus told him, "You must be born again," and expanded this to include all of us by stating quite emphatically, "Except a man be born again, he cannot see the kingdom of God" (John 3:3). Pretty dogmatic perhaps, but these are the words of Christ Himself.

Some today, like Nicodemus, will ask, 'How can a man be born when he is old? Can he enter the second time into his mother's womb, and be born? (John 3:41). But Jesus answers, "That which is born of the flesh is flesh; and that which is born of Spirit is spirit" (John 3:6), stating again that one must experience a spiritual rebirth in order to enter heaven — "You *must* be born again" (John 3:7).

Now, **have *you* been born again**? Have you experienced this spiritual rebirth? This is the one thing, according to the Bible, that will determine your eternal destiny.

So, for those who really want to know how to be born again, here is the answer from God's Word.

We must *recognize* that we are sinners, that we've all violated God's law. The Bible says, "All have sinned, and come short of the glory of God . . . There is none righteous, no, not one . . . There is not a just man upon earth, that doeth good, and sinneth not. If we say that we have no sin, we deceive ourselves, and the truth is not in us . . . If we say that we have not sinned, we make Him a liar, and His Word is not in us" (Romans 3:23, 10; Ecclesiastes 7:20; IJohn 1:8, 10).

We must *repent* of our sins. The Bible says that God 'commandeth all men everywhere to repent" (Acts 17:30). Jesus said, "Except you repent, you shall all likewise perish" (Luke 13:3). And it is not so difficult to repent as we pause to think of what our sins have cost God. It was for our sins that God, the Creator and King of this universe, left His home in heaven and came to earth in the Person of the Lord Jesus to suffer and bleed and die — that we might be forgiven. "Hereby perceive we the love of God, because He laid down His life for us" (I John 3:16). Then Jesus rose from the dead, proving His victory over sin and death.

We must *receive* Christ into our hearts and lives as our Savior. We read in the first chapter of John, speaking of the Lord Jesus, "He was in the world, and the world was made by Him, and the world knew Him not. He came unto His own, and His own received Him not. But as many as *received* Him, to them gave He power to become the sons of God, even to them that believe on His name" (John 1:10-12).

The moment we open our hearts to the Lord Jesus and place our complete trust in Him — and Him alone — as our Savior, God promises to forgive our sins, save our soul, and reserve for us a home in heaven. Then, on the authority of the Word of God, we can *know* where we'll spend eternity. God says, "These things have I written unto you that believe on the name of the Son of God; that you may *know* that you *have* eternal life" (I John 5:13). and Jesus promises, "He that heareth My word, and believeth on Him that sent Me, hath everlasting life, and shall not come into condemnation; but is passed from death unto life" (John5:24).

Now, are you willing to settle the matter of your eternal destiny? Will you do it? You can, right this moment. I sincerely hope that you will. Why not call upon the Lord right now and ask him to Save you from your sins.

Pray something like this -- Dear Lord Jesus, I confess that I am a sinner and need your forgiveness. I believe that you, Lord Jesus Christ, died for my sins and rose again from the dead. I now repent of my sins and trust only in you Christ to save me from my sins and take me to Heaven. Come into my life, forgive my sins and save my soul. Thank you for hearing my prayer. AMEN

If you trusted Christ as your personal Savior, fill in the information below and send it to us. We will send you a packet of materials that will help you to grow in your new Christian life.

WHERE WILL YOU SPEND ETERNITY?

Name _____

Address _____

City_____

State_____ Zip_____

Date_____ Phone (_____) _____

Pastor David Brown
P.O. Box 173
Oak Creek, WI 53154
Phone (414) 768-9754
E-mail: pastordavidlbrown@gmail.com

Written by Arthur DeMoss
Used by permission of The American Tract Society of Garland Texas

ABOUT THE AUTHOR

David L. Brown was born in Michigan. He came to know Christ as his Savior as the result of a Sunday school teacher throwing away the liberal curriculum, teaching through the book of Romans, and sharing the Gospel. He has been married to Linda for 49 years. She was a young lady from his home church.

David attended a Michigan University then transferred to a Christian University and Seminary where he completed a Bachelor's Degree in Social Science and Theology. He holds a Master's Degree in Theology, and Ph.D. in History, specializing in the history of the English Bible.

Since December 1979, he has been the Pastor of the First Baptist Church of Oak Creek, Wisconsin (an independent, fundamental, Baptist Church using the King James Bible and conservative music). Previous to that, he pastored an independent Baptist Church in Michigan for five years, was an assistant pastor for 4 years, and served with his wife as short term missionaries in Haiti.

Dr. Brown is the president of the *King James Bible Research Council* (www.kjbresearchcouncil.com), an organization dedicated to promoting the King James Bible and its underlying texts and other traditional text translations around the world in a solid and sensible way.

He is also the president of *Logos Communication Consortium, Inc*. (www.logosresourcepages.org), a research organization that produces a large variety of materials warning Christians of present dangers in our culture.

He is also the vice president of the *Midwest Independent Baptist Pastor's Fellowship*, a fellowship of independent Baptist pastors, missionaries, and evangelists from fourteen upper Midwest states.

Dr. Brown is the Curator of the *Christian Heritage Bible Collection* and regularly takes his rare Bible, manuscript and artifact collection to fundamental Baptist Churches teaching and preaching on the history of our English Bible, showing how God has preserved His Word(s), and why we should use the King James Bible.

He also serves as a consultant for individuals, museums, colleges, universities, and seminaries that desire to acquire or have collections of biblical manuscripts and Bibles. He is an antiquarian book dealer with contacts around the world.

He can be contacted at:
Dr. David L. Brown
8044 S. Verdev Dr.
Oak Creek, WI. 53154
Phone: 414-768-9754
Email: PastorDavidLBrown@gmail.com

www.ingramcontent.com/pod-product-compliance
Lightning Source LLC
LaVergne TN
LVHW051659080426
835511LV00017B/2642